What others are saying about
Living With Your Heart at Rest

"Often, I meet someone—and often I am that someone—whose heart shakes even when all else is still. Rarely, I meet someone —and rarely am I that someone—whose heart is still even when all else shakes. Cindy is that rare someone. She lives from a quiet and sure centre, and from that place finds strength and wisdom to handle all of life, come what may. And lucky us, now she's written about it, to help us live with hearts at rest."

~Mark Buchanan, Author of
God Speed: Walking as a Spiritual Practice

"Our hearts are, by nature, restless and unruly—frankly, we want what we want, when we want it! Taming the heart is one of the greatest challenges for any Christian who longs to grow closer to Christ. In her new book, *Living With Your Heart at Rest,* my friend Cindy Martin helps pinpoint those key heart-issues which every Christ-follower must address, helping the reader to gain a genuine heart for Christ. If your heart's desire is to replace your willful determinations with godly pursuits, then this is the book for you!"

~Joni Eareckson Tada, Joni and Friends
International Disability Center

"With frank honesty Cindy shares life-tested principles that will help you break free from the frenzied life into deep soul rest that only God provides. Saturated in Scripture and packed with the practical, *Living With Your Heart at Rest* is like mining for gold … and actually finding some."

~Phil Callaway, speaker and author
of *Laughing Matters*

"It's rare to come across a book that offers original and compelling ideas that both instruct and inspire you. Cindy's book is one of those that I passionately recommend to you. She will draw you in and guide you into this insightful exploration fueled by her pastoral warmth and spiritual authority mingled with personal brokenness and authenticity. Cindy writes from her deep experience and masterfully weaves a colourful tapestry of pertinent scriptures, stories, and practical exhortations of what it means to live with a heart at rest in God. I need this!"

~Roger Helland, District Minister, Baptist General Conference in Alberta, and author of *The Devout Life, Magnificent Surrender,* and *Missional Spirituality*

"Right is the middle of the busyness and struggles of our lives, Jesus promises that our hearts can find rest. Yet often we do not seem to experience what we long for. It has been my privilege to walk with Cindy Martin as she lives a life that is incredibly full, yet has come to know the reality of a restful heart. In her book, *Living With Your Heart at Rest,* Cindy shows through examples in her life and truths found in Scripture that it is possible to find that rest. Through the pages of this book you will discover God's desire for you to experience that to the full."

~Dr. Henry Schorr, Senior Pastor of Centre Street Church

"Cindy Martin is out to prove that the words found in John 10:10, 'I have come that they may have life, and that they may have it more abundantly,' are true. She wants her readers to recognize rest is available, a deep soul rest that will change the way you encounter everyday life. *Living With Your Heart At Rest* is your invitation to live the life of abundance and experience rest at the same time.

Cindy Martin takes you on a journey leading you to understand how to navigate through a number of heart stages including the skeptical heart, the stony heart, the strong heart, the surrendered heart, and arriving in the place of the sacred heart.

To embark on this journey, she provides the reader practical tools based on a clear understanding of biblical principles and personal experience—experience that has given her a realization of the depth of God's love. I encourage you to read this book and put Cindy Martin's techniques to work for you. You will discover that you can have rest that will result in a heart filled with hope."

~Gerry Wakeland, Women's Ministry Leader and Spiritual Director

Living With Your Heart at Rest

Living with Your Heart at Rest

Cindy Martin

Bold Vision Books
PO Box 2011
Friendswood, Texas 77549

Dedication

To my late grandma, Esther Henderson, whose spiritual legacy still lingers in my mind. Thank you for teaching me how to pray and instilling a love for God's Word in my heart.

Table of Contents

Acknowledgments

Walter, my faith-filled husband, whose belief in me never wavered.

Randy & Autumn, my precious adult children, who have taught me much about grace and truth.

My mom, Ruth, whose love for me has been tireless.

Rosemary, who helped unlock my dreams as a writer and speaker.

Barb, whose wisdom and exhortation continue to impact me deeply.

Karen, Deborah, Elizabeth, Kathy and Diane who have held my heart and labored in prayer on my behalf.

A host of friends, neighbors and colleagues who have helped me to see Jesus and experience His love through their lives.

Bold Vision Books – thank you for your patience in teaching me what I didn't even know I didn't know.

Introduction

Writing about living with your heart at rest flows out of my personal journey. It has resulted in a passionate desire welling up inside me to help people to understand the difference Jesus makes in their everyday lives. This book will not necessarily provide quick easy solutions to your current situation or even answer all your questions. Rather it is an invitation to encounter God *in this life*. It is my prayer that God would so renew your mind that you would understand and live convinced that His presence, power and provision are just as real as the harsh realities you face.

When we live with that as our core conviction and learn to invite God into our moments, everything is different. We see things from a fresh perspective and we experience the whole of our lives in a way that defies the emptiness and loss of purpose that characterizes many of the people that sit in our churches today. When we are utterly convinced of God's goodness, our faith comes alive. It becomes authentic, relevant and life-giving. Our souls are anchored and given wings simultaneously and it is glorious! We begin to see how we were meant to live as children of Almighty God, living our lives with clarity and confidence as hope rises from within our hearts. Oh, that we would live the lives that Jesus died to provide!

Chapter One

The Significant Heart: Transforming the Way You View Yourself

My guess is that you picked up this book because you desire to live with your heart at rest. But the circumstances of your life make the idea of sustainable, deep soul-anchoring rest seem elusive, if not out of reach. Or perhaps the title intrigued you but inwardly you thought, *that's impossible.*

Whatever the reason, I propose that God has orchestrated the events of your life so that you could spend some time reading and reflecting in response to an often-undetected craving in your heart that you may struggle to articulate. That niggling undercurrent of discontent that badgers your thoughts and plagues your emotions as it begs for answers to questions like, "Is this as good as it gets?" "Why can't I sense God's power or presence in my life?" "How does my faith *actually* sustain me in the tough times?"

I invite you to consider the prospect that not only is it possible to live with your heart at rest, but by mining the treasures revealed throughout the pages of Scripture, you can learn to make heart rest part of your daily experience. Join me as we explore what living with our hearts at rest looks like and then discover how living that way can permeate every area of our lives.

What is a Heart at Rest?

Living with our hearts at rest comes as a subtle but vital shift takes place in the posture of our heart. That shift comes as we learn to invite God into our moments—both the monumental and the mundane. Sounds simplistic. Maybe even naïve. I assure you that simple does not mean easy. Just as child-like faith does not come naturally to adults, neither does purposefully extending an invitation to the Creator of the universe to be part of our day-to-day happenings. Albeit unintentional, this omission is the 'missing piece' that, until rediscovered and re-engaged, is at the source of what fuels the emptiness of our soul and feeds the disillusionment we feel with our faith.

Plain and simple, living with your heart at rest is finding God to be enough ... no matter what. It is that almost undefinable anchor that brings uncommon perspective and undeniable hope to any situation we may face. In our marriages. Our parenting. Our relationships. Our struggles. Our desire for real honest–to–goodness joy. Psalm 62 says, "My soul finds rest in God alone." I admit, at first glance resting in God alone can seem like a pie in the sky idea. We rarely see this kind of rest modeled in our society, never mind our churches, homes, or families. In fact, the notion of a heart at rest is not usually even on our radar screens until we've exhausted our resources and reached out in desperation asking God for the impossible.

This concept of living with your heart at rest is precipitated by one simple truth that I believe is foundational to the Christian faith. For reasons unknown to me, this truth has not only been overlooked, but seemingly and sadly, dismissed and forgotten. The truth is this—your heart matters. You, the *real* you, all pretense stripped aside, barefoot and unrefined, matters to Almighty God. Your heart encompasses not only your emotions, but also your mind and your will. It is your soul, the very core of your being. The sum total of *your* unique personality, hopes, dreams, thoughts, decisions, failures, strengths, weaknesses, insecurities and successes, they all comprise your heart, and they *all* matter to God.

I can almost hear some of you laughing in cynicism and disbelief. Your heart has been deeply wounded by the harsh realities of living in a world broken by sin, and the pain you carry in your heart is living proof of how deeply broken our world really is. I want you to know that there is hope.

In the pages that follow, we are going to take a candid look at the source of our restless hearts and discover practical and sustainable ways to bring our hearts to a place of uncommon rest. There are no magic formulas. Like a butterfly emerging from the confines of its cocoon, part of the journey to living with your heart at rest will involve struggle. Still, I promise you, no matter the depth of your pain or the emptiness of your soul and regardless of failed attempts to do better or figure things out, God extends this invitation to you, "Come, My child; there is a better way to live."

Signs of a Restless Heart

We often learn to live out of our heads instead of our hearts in response to the happenings and inevitable hardships in our lives. Initially this strategy may seem effective, but eventually, our hearts become restless. Our hearts no longer bow to the demands from our head and as if suffocating, they clamor to be acknowledged and addressed. There are a few tell-tale symptoms of a restless heart. Take a look at the list in the acronym below, and see if you recognize any of these symptoms in your life.

R—regularly angry or fearful. While Scripture definitely speaks of healthy fear and righteous anger, it also speaks clearly and strongly against rage, harsh words, and paralyzing fear.

E—entitled mindset. An entitled heart is filled with expectations *of* others (spouse, children, friends, church and God) and *for* myself (what I deserve).

S—selfish/striving; hard to please; impatient. Not much explanation required. If in doubt, ask your family or anyone in your closest sphere of influence.

T—trust no one; lone ranger. Be wise in whom you trust with your heart, but trusting no one leaves God out too. Alone is indeed a lonely place to be.

L—loss of satisfaction with life; disillusioned with God. These feelings are usually fostered and accompanied by feelings of being trapped, disconnected, and powerless in our circumstances.

E—envious. Our hearts become increasingly restless as we focus on all we don't have and when we **choose** not to develop an attitude of gratitude for what we do have.

S—stingy with money, compliments and extending grace. The more restless our hearts, the more inward our focus.

S—self-doubt; second guessing yourself; insecure. Doubt is often the result of believing the enemy's lies about ourselves, our circumstances, or God's desire and ability to change situations.

If you recognized any of the above as recurring symptoms in your life, you may have a spiritual heart condition common among Christians and non-Christians alike—restless heart syndrome. While the syndrome is common, its treatment isn't. We can no longer do common activities and expect uncommon results. In the pages ahead, we will examine solid, practical and biblical principles outlining God's design for living with our hearts at rest. Before we unpack those principles, let's be sure we clearly understand our end goal.

What a Heart at Rest Is Not

In future chapters, we will discuss some of these common counterfeits for living with our hearts at rest:

- Living in denial
- Faking it
- Living like a monk in an "ohm" state

- Tuning out on life with the grim resignation that this is as good as it gets
- Having everything under control—finally getting organized
- Image/sin management
- Living solely out of our heads instead of in tandem with our hearts

In order to effectively dive into the practice of living with our heart at rest, we first need to understand why God places so much importance on our heart.

Your Heart Matters

It is a well-accepted fact that our hearts are at the core of our physical existence. When our heart is functioning as it should, it becomes the source from which the rest of our body draws its lifeblood. However, when it's malfunctioning, we can encounter a variety of ailments that demand to be addressed. And left un-attended, the heart will, with haunting finality, stop ... and then nothing else will matter. Simply stated, when it comes to our physical well-being, we cannot engage in a meaningful life without a functioning heart.

The same is true of our spiritual well-being. Before we can engage in a meaningful discussion about living with our hearts at rest, we must first grasp the depth of this simple but transforming truth—your heart matters. The word "heart" is used over 500 times throughout the pages of scripture and more than 60 times in the book of Proverbs alone.[1] It is mentioned more often than faith, money, or even love.[2] Our hearts *really* do matter to God. Of all the ideas He could have included in the Bible, God determined that a deep understanding of the value of our hearts was of paramount importance. Why?

The book of Proverbs is bursting with pages of practical wisdom instructing us on how to *do life* on almost every level and yet Proverbs 4:23 tells us that "**Above all else**, guard your heart for it is the well spring of life" [Emphasis mine]. Above all else—if we understand nothing else, we need to know how much our hearts matter to God. The Message Bible translates the verse this way, "Keep vigilant watch over your heart; that's where life starts."

The heart is where life starts.

Just as it is with our physical heart, so it is with our spiritual heart. That core of our being is where we draw the lifeblood we need to engage in and sustain our spiritual life.

Beyond its role as the organ that pumps blood and oxygen throughout our bodies, the heart is also used to describe "the whole personality including intellectual and emotional functions or traits"[3] Yet in the spiritual realm, "the word *heart* means more than mental or emotional capacity; it also encompasses one's values."[4] It forms the basis of our morality and is the source from which we draw our perceptions, attitudes, and thought processes. We think, talk, and act based on what is in our heart. If the way we think impacts the way we act, it logically follows that we can change the way we act if we change the way we think. I believe the "renewing of the mind" referenced in Romans 12 includes a (sometimes radical) change of heart. As Dallas Willard puts it, "You can live opposite of what you profess, but you can't live opposite of what you believe."[5] Changing what we believe begins by filling our minds with God's truth. Filling our minds with God's truth is key to impacting our heart's beliefs. As His truth penetrates our hearts, it results in a change in our behavior. When our heart's beliefs are in alignment with God's truth, we can live with our hearts at rest. What we do in word and deed is a product of what are we on the inside.

Take some time to reflect on these thoughts and ponder the scripture passages below, allowing God to speak to you about the value of your heart.

Our Heart is Where

We accept or reject God.

"For it is with your heart that you believe and are justified, and it is with your mouth that you confess and are saved" (Romans 10:10).

"The fool says in his heart, 'There is no God'" (Psalm 14:1).

Wisdom makes its home.

"Wisdom reposes in the heart of the discerning (Proverbs 14:33).

"Whoever obeys His command will come to no harm, and the wise heart will know the proper time and procedure" (Ecclesiastes 8:5). See also Proverbs 3:1.

Values originate.

"For where your treasure is, there your heart will be also" (Matthew 6:21).

"The good man brings good things out of the good stored up in his heart, and the evil man brings evil things out of the evil stored up in his heart" (Luke 6:45a).

Trust/faith originate.

"Trust in the LORD with all your heart and lean not on your own understanding" (Proverbs 3:5). Faith and trust start in our hearts not our heads. See also Mark 11:23.

Words originate.

"For out of the overflow of his heart his mouth speaks" (Luke 6:45b).

"But the things that come out of the mouth come from the heart" (Matthew 15:18). See also Matthew 12:34 and Psalm 19:14).

Decisions are made.

"In his heart, a man plans his course, but the LORD determines his steps" (Proverbs 16:9).

"Each man should give what he has decided in his heart to give" (2 Corinthians 9:7). See also Proverbs 19:21.

We hold our capacity to love God and others.

"Love the LORD your God with all your heart ..." (Deuteronomy 6:5), See also Matthew 22:37, Mark 12:30, Luke 10:27. Notice that it's mentioned first as a matter of priority.

"I will search for the one my heart loves" (Song of Solomon 3:2).

The basis for judgment is found.

"I, the LORD, search the heart and examine the mind, to reward a man according to his conduct, according to what his deeds deserve" (Jeremiah 17:10; 11:20).

"Does not He who weighs the heart perceive it? Does not He who guards your life know it? Will He not repay each person according to what he has done? (Proverbs 24:12).

"For the word of God is living and active. Sharper than any double-edged sword, it penetrates even to dividing soul and spirit, joints and marrow; it judges the thoughts and attitudes of the heart" (Hebrews 4:12).

Your heart can also:

Forget.

"Only be careful, and watch yourselves closely so that you do not forget the things your eyes have seen or let them slip from your heart as long as you live. Teach them to your children and to their children after them" (Deuteronomy 4:9).

Become anxious.

"Do not be anxious about anything …" (Philippians 4:6).

"So then, banish anxiety from your heart and cast off the troubles of your body" (Ecclesiastes 11:10).

Become discouraged.

"My days have passed, my plans are shattered, and so are the desires of my heart" (Job 17:11).

"Be careful, keep calm and don't be afraid. Do not lose heart …" (Isaiah 7:4).

Become proud.

"By your great skill in trading you have increased your wealth, and because of your wealth your heart has grown proud" (Ezekiel 28:5).

"The pride of your heart has deceived you" (Obadiah 1:3).

"Before his downfall a man's heart is proud, but humility comes before honor" (Proverbs 18:12).

Be divided.

"I will give them an undivided heart" (Ezekiel 11:19).

Harbor idols.

"… Sets up idols in his heart" (Ezekiel 14:7).

Impact your physical health.

"A heart at peace gives life to the body, but envy rots the bones" (Proverbs 14:30).

Be deceived.

"Their heart is deceitful, and now they must bear their guilt" (Hosea 10:2).

"The heart is deceitful above all things …" (Jeremiah 17:9).

Be tested.

"… to humble you and to test you in order to know what was in your heart, whether or not you would keep His commands" (Deuteronomy 8:2).

Be broken.

"My heart is broken within me" (Jeremiah 23:9).

"A broken and contrite heart, O God, you will not despise" (Psalm 51:17).

Be known by God.

"Lord, you know everyone's heart" (Act 1:24).

"God, who knows the heart, showed that He accepted them by giving the Holy Spirit to them" (Acts 15:8).

"Would not God have discovered it, since He knows the secrets of the heart?" (Psalm 44:21).

Be changed.

"As Saul turned to leave Samuel, God changed Saul's heart …" (1 Samuel 10:9).

"… get a new heart and a new spirit …" (Ezekiel 18:31).

"Create in me a pure heart, O God, and renew a steadfast spirit within me" (Psalm 51:10).

Be revived.

"I live in a high and holy place … to revive the spirit of the lowly and to revive the heart of the contrite" (Isaiah 57:15).

While this list isn't exhaustive, we can begin to see why we are instructed to "guard our hearts." Webster's defines the word "guard" as, "1) to protect from danger; defend. 2) to watch over so as to prevent escape, disclosure, or indiscretion. 3) to attempt to prevent (an opponent) from playing effectively or scoring."[6] In light of what we've learned from Scripture about our hearts, this definition fits. Knowing our heart can become anxious, proud, and impact our physical health, we need to protect it from that danger. Knowing that our heart can forget, harbor idols, and be divided, we need to give focused attention so as to "prevent the escape, disclosure or indiscretion." And knowing that Satan, the great enemy of our souls is constantly attacking our hearts in an attempt to discourage and deceive, we need to be attentive to our hearts so that he is not able to play effectively or gain a foothold.

I hope you noticed that even though there are many negative dangers to our hearts, there are also some positive results when we effectively guard our hearts. Guarding our hearts involves not only what we keep out of them but also what we put into them. In subsequent chapters we will be "putting skin" on some strategies that encompass both parts of guarding our hearts.

As I mentioned earlier, my observation has been that many people shut their hearts off (or at least parts of them), and live out of their heads because it just seems easier. Yet, you can only close off so many parts of your heart until all that's left is a shell. There have been times in my life when my heart very closely resembled a shell. In fact, at a particularly low point, I wrote the following words:

My Head and Heart Aren't Talking

I know what I believe, I've known it from the start
But in these heavy days, I can't get buy-in from my heart
Every time I think I'm starting to see the light and get up
off the ground
Another wave comes along, and the battle goes to another
round.
Most days it seems I'm winning the battle for my mind
But when it comes to connecting my heart – it's flat lined

I want to move on and not feel like the walking dead
Yet I seem so powerless in making my heart line up with
my head
I no longer feel the need to be perpetually strong 'cause I've
seen how weak I've really become
I just want to feel again and not be so incredibly numb!
If I knew what to do, I would have done it by now

But I don't even know the what - not to mention the how
I know that life won't always be like this and one day I
will make it up this hill
But it won't be because of some false hope or a tiny white
pill
I don't think I'm too good for the hard stuff or that I
should even be immune,
But God, could you send some encouragement?
And please, let it be soon!

Indeed, it was a dark time in my life, and I wanted the chaos inside me to stop. The floodgate of pain that had swallowed up my life was forcing me to live out of my heart instead of just my head. No longer could my head convince my heart that everything was OK.

I did make it up the hill and it wasn't because of false hope or a tiny white pill. However, I'm not suggesting that those who need medication don't take it. God came and met me in my pain and did in my heart what I was powerless to do on my own.

Rite of Passage

I've observed that pain serves as a rite of passage as we learn to live with our hearts at rest. Deep heart-level pain is often seen as something to be avoided at all costs. However, God uses our pain for good as He relentlessly pursues what He wants more than anything else—our hearts. As this truth penetrates through the pain in our lives, it provides the anchor that allows us to change the way we look at ourselves, our life, and our Lord. *The degree to which we trust God will be the degree to which we experience rest for our souls.* Friends, trusting God is not easy. If it was, more people would be doing it and doing it well. If this kind of trust is starting to seem a little (or a lot!) scary, please remember, you cannot be brave until you're scared first.

As we grapple with this issue together, looking through the lens of Scripture, we will come to see that the depth of God's goodness is why He is worth trusting with all our hearts.

Re-Engaging Our Heart

I believe that it's much easier to think through our struggles than it is to feel through them. I'm not saying that it's not hard work trying to think of a solution to a problem or even that you shouldn't consider your options, but have you ever tried to embrace a difficult situation that you were in and allow yourself to feel all the emotions that come with it? I suspect that for most of us, we would find feeling in the depths of our heart to be a bigger struggle. We would rather spend our energy *doing* something to fix the problem instead of engaging our hearts.

Our minds have told our hearts that they can't do what hearts are supposed to do—that is to feel. Instead, our mind analyzes and strategizes to the point that the mind paralyzes our heart, and then we wonder why we *feel* so empty. We live in a society that has saturated our thinking processes but has done very little to care for our hearts. We are inundated with the pressure to learn and do more faster and better than the next person so we can rise above them. Often those that do allow their hearts to feel through the stuff of life are marginalized as too emotional or irrational and sometimes just plain lazy.

Now let me be clear, there is such a thing as wallowing in the emotion of a situation. And yes, some people let their emotions rule their lives. Overwhelmed emotions cripple their ability to think clearly. I'm not suggesting we allow emotion to rule, and there definitely is a time to move on. However, many people try to bury or outrun their pain instead of addressing it.

I believe the reason for such a calculated approach to our lives is that we don't honestly believe that our individual hearts matter to God. Perhaps as it relates to salvation and sanctification, we might give mental ascent to the idea, but on a day-to-day basis, that spiritual reality and its implications are foreign to many, even (and maybe especially) those within the church. We use expressions like Jesus as the Lover of our soul and the Lifter of our head. Do we *really* know what those titles mean? What does Him being Lover and Lifter feel like? Have you experienced Him in the chaos and crises of *your* life? Often, it's not until we have exhausted all of our human strategies and resources in an attempt to control what God never intended to be in our control that we even consider there is another way to live. We can't continue relying on our habitual coping mechanisms, thinking that they will be enough to change our circumstances or our perspective. We need Divine enablement. Said another way, we can't keep doing common things and expect uncommon results. Often the first step is to learn what we need to unlearn. That will be our focus in chapter three, but first let me share my story of learnings and unlearnings.

Key Learnings:

- Your heart *matters*. Your **heart** matters. **Your** heart matters. Ask God to let that truth soak your soul like a slow, gentle rain.
- When your heart's beliefs are in alignment with God's truth, you can live with your heart at rest.
- The degree to which you trust God will be the degree to which you live with your heart at rest.
- You can't be brave unless you're scared first.
- You can't keep doing common things and expect uncommon results.

Questions to Consider:

1. What signs of a restless heart do you see in your life?

2. Of the functions/capacities of the heart discussed, which ones stand out to you? Why? Were there any "aha" moments for you?

3. Reflect on Dallas Willard's statement, "You can live opposite of what you profess, but you can't live opposite of what you believe." What are the areas of alignment/misalignment that you see in your life?

4. Where do you see your heart's beliefs out of alignment with God's truth?

5. What does the phrase, "Jesus, Lover of my soul" mean to you?

Passages to Ponder:

"Above all else, guard your heart, for everything you do flows from it " (Proverbs 4:23 NIV).

"Keep vigilant watch over your heart; that's where life starts" (Proverbs 4:23 The Message).

Prayer of Invitation:

Lord Jesus,
Thank You that my heart matters so much to You. Help me to better understand the value You place on my heart. Give me strength and the desire to bring my heart's beliefs in alignment with Your truth. Teach me to invite You into my moments. Grant me the courage I need to be brave.
In the strong and powerful name of Jesus, Amen.

Practice Point:

Review the passages on the value of your heart and reflect on those verses that stood out to you.

Many of us have an unconscious routine that we follow when we shower. For example, right arm first, then left arm, then right leg, left leg, etc. We don't even think about it, we just do it. The same is true when it comes to our spiritual routines. We do or don't do certain routines as a matter of habit. As we move toward living with our hearts at rest, we will need to make changes. As a way to practice in the physical realm what we will need to do in the spiritual realm, my challenge is for you to change up your shower routine. If you wash your right arm first, try washing your left arm first, etc.

It is supposed to feel unnatural, and it will take longer. As you're doing it, be mindful of how much extra effort it takes, especially at first. Making changes in our spiritual lives will seem awkward and initially take more time, too. As you work to develop a new shower routine, reflect on how the retraining of our brain may be similar to the retraining of our hearts.

Chapter Two

The Skeptical Heart: Moving from Overwhelmed to Authentic

When I share my story, I often feel like people only hear the difficult happenings of my life and feel a sense of sympathy or pity for me. While God has definitely used the hard moments to shape me, I invite you not to focus on the troublesome events but to look beneath it all and see God's relentless pursuit of my heart. Notice how He used the earlier seasons of my life to prepare me for what was yet to come.

The Journey of a Rising Pharisee

Straight from the pages of a fairy tale, I was born into a home that dearly loved me and cared for me. Even though my brother, who is 15 months older than me, said, "nice puppy, nice puppy" when I arrived home from the hospital, I soon found my spot as the princess of our home and the apple of my dad's eye. We enjoyed a closeness as a family that I've since learned is not common. I grew up in what I now understand to be a rather poor home, though at the time I didn't see it that way. Living on the farm with animals to butcher and a huge garden meant there was always enough to eat, along with extra to share with others. My parents worked hard to keep their bills paid, but almost always when my brother or I would ask for something, we would hear, "We can't afford it." I remember one day as a young child persistently asking my mom for a quarter to buy candy and finally, in exasperation she exclaimed, "You can't have a quarter because I only have seven cents!" I remember how deeply that penetrated my mind and heart and birthed a lack mentality that would plague me for many years. I came to learn in later years that much of my parents' lack was due to them being swindled out of tens of thousands of dollars. I also learned that news of my mother's pregnancy with me was not met with great anticipation by some who didn't think my parents could afford to have another baby. The disappointment was intensified when they found out I was a girl. Yet for the most part my young years were ones of security, filled with fun and laughter, as I was blissfully oblivious to the underlying tension and turmoil.

My dad had a seemingly endless supply of old vehicles and tractors so our yard became one big outdoor playground. My brother used to like to play with all the animals while I definitely did not. I was much happier helping out in the house, so I learned to cook and clean at an early age. As my mom worked outside the home, I started (under my mom's detailed instructions) to make our family Christmas Eve dinners when I was 10 years old. My mom was always so thankful when I would tidy the house or clean out some cupboards, so in my young mind, I subconsciously surmised that accomplishing something was the way to get her approval. I've grown to realize that her appreciation was a reflection of her gratitude for helping lighten her very heavy load. I was deeply loved simply because I was her daughter.

I was privileged to have my maternal grandmother play a significant role in my life. She lost her husband and oldest son (my grandpa and uncle) in two separate car accidents 11 days apart, over Christmas, the year after my parents were married. Yet she was passionately in love with Jesus, and her relentless faith and commitment to Christ impacted my life deeply—long after the day she would forever enter the presence of the One she loved so dearly. The wisdom of her words still lingers in my mind to this day. I was seven years old when I gave my heart to Jesus in her backyard. When I was 10 years old, she signed me up with the Bible Memory Association to memorize seven Bible verses each week. Every Thursday I would come by her house after school and recite that week's verses. In the process, she passed on her love for God's Word and its power in our lives. Upon reflecting on her life, I see now that she followed the model of Christ by answering the happenings of life with Scripture.

My grandma lived in town, and we lived in the country, so I would often stay overnight at her house because of school activities. It was during those overnight visits at her house that she began to impart and pass on her spiritual legacy. I could not leave the house in the morning until she had prayed over me. When our little church was without a pastor, Wednesday night prayer meetings often meant that the only people that were in attendance were my grandma, Aunt Louisa and Mrs. Francis—three godly widows who poured out their hearts before God and upheld the ministry of the church before the throne of grace. It was an amazing privilege whenever I could be there with them. I learned much about the power and practice of prayer from these precious women.

Bible camp had always been a highlight of my summer and constituted my vacation as dad worked in road construction as well as working on the farm, so there was no time to get away for a family holiday. (Not to mention, "We couldn't afford it.") I loved camp and took seriously the messages presented. My faith was becoming my own. I was baptized at summer camp when I was 12 years old.

While my early childhood years were quite idyllic, my life changed when I entered junior high, and in a word, it was awful. I was an honor student and a Christian—neither of which made me very popular. My classmates were very cruel. The physical shoving into lockers was painful, but their words hurt much more. They twisted words I said, bombarding me with insults, usually filled with sexual innuendo and sometimes just plain filth. Then they would taunt me, asking if God was going to zap them for what they had just said to me.

It was during those years that the Pharisee in me began to rise up and gain momentum. Determined to not be tainted by their influence or further wounded by their words, I resolved to go it alone—just me and God. My parents walked distantly from the Lord at that time so I didn't feel I could talk with them, and my brother had begun a season of rebellion that consumed a lot of their time and energy. I talked with my grandmother, but I think I was too embarrassed to tell her about what the kids at school said. Thus, the Lone Ranger in me picked up speed. I lived for Friday night youth group at our church and the chance to be with other people my age who accepted me.

Our home began to change as well. My parents argued often about the best way to deal with my brother's choices. I spent a lot of energy trying to cover up or put a positive spin on the realities of my family and school life. There seemed to be little time for my issues, and I dared not be the straw that broke the camel's back. My parents tried to hide the depths of my brother's rebellion from me. Even though their plan was well intentioned for sure, not knowing further isolated me. I felt like my thoughts and feelings didn't matter.

The mantle of spiritual leadership for our home seemed to have no place to land, and while I was never asked to carry it, I definitely felt the weight of it. With that came the (often self-imposed) expectation that I would always make the right choices and that I needed to be counted on to be the good kid and reflect my family in a good light. After I had moved away from home, God drew my parents into a much closer relationship with Him, but during that season of my life, I learned that it was much easier to live out of my head than it was to live out of my heart.

To Do and Not to Be

Well, I guess you could say that I was cradled in independence. Being the only girl in the family and having both parents working outside the home meant that I was required to become quite responsible at a young age. My mother was a strong, capable woman, and she expected nothing less than that from me. For the most part, that suited me just fine. My independent nature flourished. I didn't have to share my ideas with anyone else or have to listen to the input of others. However, there was much subconscious input to be had. My dad always said, "Do what you do well," and his insecurity over not finishing high school and the notion that city people were just smarter than us country folk significantly impacted my way of thinking. Also, I rarely saw my parents rest. They usually worked until it was time to collapse into bed. We did enjoy fun, family times together, but laziness was simply not tolerated.

James 1:22 was my life verse for many years, "be ye doers of the word and not hearers only." And do I did. I went to a private Christian school for high school which allowed students to work at their own pace. I graduated from high school a year early and then went to Bible College and completed my Bachelor of Religious Education degree by the time I was 20. I graduated with a 4.0 GPA and received the Governor General's award. I served as a resident assistant, held a position on student council and in my fourth year was the Assistant Dorm Supervisor for all of the resident students. I trust you're able to see behind the accomplishments to the extreme pressure I had placed myself under. I had very high expectations for myself and unfortunately, for others as well.

Our church preached the crucified life of Galatians 2:20 with much vigor. "I am crucified with Christ; yet not I but Christ Who lives in me." The truths I learned at that season of my life have been foundational to my walk with God and continue to profoundly impact my thinking and approach to life. I glommed onto those truths, determined to excel at my interpretation (or misinterpretation) of what really mattered in life—*getting things right*. While the crucified life was not taught this way, I had somehow picked up the notion that the crucified life meant consistently saying, doing, and thinking the right things. Basically, getting as close to perfection as a human being could this side of heaven. However, not much emphasis was ever put on the role of grace—receiving it or extending it. I never understood the balance of living in the tension between what is and what will one day be.

We were taught to stifle our accomplishments and never seek the limelight, as those were all evidences of pride. I loved to teach and lead. I was regularly invited to use my gifts and abilities, but I did not always feel free to do so in the way I believed God wired me. I felt again as I often have throughout my life—different from everyone else, kind of like the words to the Sesame Street song, "one of these things is not like the other." *Why did God make me this way? Why didn't other people love Him and want to live for Him like I did? Why couldn't I serve Him the way He made me?* The disconnect between my ideal world and my reality was growing, and because I couldn't make sense of it, the Pharisee in me grew larger and more powerful.

I moved back home after Bible College, informally engaged to a man I had been dating for two years while at school. He had been the student body president, and we were the supposed model couple. We had bought our wedding rings and planned for a September wedding with the intentions of moving to the West Coast to work in full time ministry. Long story short, the relationship ended, and I started working at a local grocery store believing I was destined to be a single missionary in Africa. My striving heart was empty. I wondered which way to turn.

As is often the case, God had a plan I could never thought of on my own. I met Walter (who is now my husband) through a mutual friend, but was certain that he could not be the man for me. After all, he was younger than me, he had hair as long as mine and he had aspirations of being a pig farmer. *How could this possibly be God's plan?* Not only that, when I first met him, he seemed far from God. In His mercy, God orchestrated the events of Walter's life to bring him back to Himself. Sadly, one of those events was the death of his older brother as a result of a car accident two months before his brother's long anticipated wedding day. Through that season of sorrow, I had the privilege of seeing the depth of his spiritual heritage and his personal turning back to God. Still, I resisted the idea of him as husband material. However, after receiving God's confirmation, our relationship moved forward. We were married on July 1, 1989.

We became involved with our church and shortly after we were married, we spent some time traveling with The Sutera Twins and Canadian Revival Fellowship. We served as prayer room leaders and had the privilege of seeing God transform many people's lives as He released them from the bondages they carried. We, too, were released of some of the burdens we carried. That teaching and those experiences have been foundational in the deepening of our faith. Due in part to our time with Canadian Revival Fellowship, the desire welled up in Walter to go to Bible College. We moved to Prairie Bible College in Three Hills, Alberta, Canada in the spring of 1992, and Walter started taking spring sessions. For the next three years, I served as Secretary to the Dean and Academic Dean of the College. While we were there (when I was 25 years old), I was asked to serve as the Married Student Advisor to the 105 married student families that made up our close-knit married student community. I was so surprised to be asked to serve in that capacity as I definitely didn't feel qualified for the position. In the days to come, I would see God's shaping hand on my life as a result of that role.

The Valley of the Shadow of Death

My parents modeled a fiercely independent outlook on life. Their motto might well have been, "figure it out or go without." This way of thinking resonated within me and served to fuel the flame of independence burning within me.

I had decided early in life that needing help was a sign of weakness, and so I lived several years of my life thinking that my faith, my husband, and myself were really all I needed. I never had a sister, so the idea of just talking with other women for no apparent reason didn't make sense to me. It seemed to me that many women I'd met were so emotional and squishy that I often wondered why God hadn't made me a man. I was frequently annoyed by other women and was often impatient and irritated with those who seemed to be distracting me from getting my work done with all their emotional neediness. Compassion was not my forte. I had steeled my heart. God knew much tenderizing was needed.

I realize that some might say that from a spiritual perspective, I lived a charmed life during my growing up years. I was in church from the first Sunday I came home from the hospital. Cradle role, Sunday School, Pioneer Girls, youth group, Bible college--it all seemed so black and white. After all, God was good, and the Bible said to trust Him, so I wondered, why were people having such a hard time trusting Him? Well, it was in my later 20s and early 30s that things seemed to fade from black and white into a thick cloud of grey. God lovingly but painfully showed me that there was a better way to live.

After being married for 3 or 4 years, Walter and I decided it was time to have a family, but God had other plans. After 3 confirmed miscarriages, but quite likely more, we underwent extensive testing only to be told that we had unexplained infertility. Not only could they not explain the difficulty in conceiving, they were also unable to determine why when I did conceive, I was only able to carry the baby for a matter of weeks before it would self abort.

Regime after regime of fertility drugs failed to produce their anticipated result. As I sat all alone in the chair where I regularly came to meet with God in the early hours of the morning, I asked Him what I had done that He would pass over me month after month, year after year. Like Hannah in the Old Testament, I begged God to grant me the insatiable desire in my heart for a child.

My husband's family was prolific when it came to 'being fruitful and multiplying.' He is the youngest of ten children and at the time we were married, we already had nieces and nephews numbering in the double digits with many more to come. In my mind I just knew people were blaming me, thinking I was so focused on pursuing a career that I didn't have time for a baby. I started blaming me too. I felt like such a disappointment to people. There were teenage girls getting pregnant all around me – yet the little booties we had bought on our honeymoon in anticipation of our future baby had no little feet to fill them so they remained tucked away in my hope chest—hoping that maybe one day …

This took place while we were still at Prairie Bible College, during the time of my role as the Married Student Advisor. Part of the responsibility of that role was to visit new moms in the hospital after the birth of their children. After each visit, I grappled with why God wouldn't let me be the one being visited instead of always being the one celebrating with someone else.

My faith was further tested through the process of three failed adoptions--the birth mothers chose to keep their babies, some of them at the last minute. The anguish of dashed hopes had me wondering if God really cared or what had I done to deserve all this pain.

In October of 1995, we entered another adoption scenario. This one proved to be successful, yet nothing like we expected or were prepared for. Arrangements had been made for me to be in the delivery room to watch our child be born in early January. However, Christmas night of 1995, we got a call telling us it was time. We raced to the hospital located in a city two hours from where we were living, with our hearts in a state of reckless abandon, pounding like marathon runners getting their first glimpse of the finish line. The realization of our dream was in sight, but all too soon, it faded into a nightmare. The woman who desired to gift us with our son, suffered significant complications during delivery, and as a result both she and the baby were flown by air ambulances to larger hospitals in hopes their lives could be spared. Walter and I stood by the window, our noses pressed against the glass like forgotten puppies, watching in disbelief as the helicopter lifted off. Overcome by shock and looming devastation, I held onto the nearby railing as my knees no longer supported me. Numb and depleted, I remember asking, "God, why does it have to be so hard to have a baby?"

Turmoil churned in my heart as we drove to the NICU (Neonatal Intensive Care Unit) at the hospital that our son, Randy (named after his uncle that died in the car accident), had been taken to. I was too overwhelmed to cry. My do-er personality was powerless to do anything, and I sat in a heap, drowning in feelings of disbelief, feeling betrayed by God and hopeless. Each mile we drove, my heart grew increasingly anxious as I wondered if Randy would still be alive when we got there. What if he's not? *God, You wouldn't allow that to happen to us, after all we've been through, would You? I know life isn't supposed to be easy, but this is so hard. I don't know if I can do this. It's not supposed to happen this way.* As nervous tension accelerated through my body, I rocked back and forth, exasperated by my inability to fix the situation. I stared out the window of our car wondering if I was destined to travel down the road of empty arms once again.

I scolded God. *You know, God, this baby is Your child. You made him and it's Your job to take care of him.* The unspoken but unmistakable reply that came to my heart was immediate.

"I know it's My job…please let Me do it."

At that moment, I had a choice. Continue to harden my heart and go my way or invite His power and presence to meet the needs of my overwhelmed heart. The internal wrestle was fierce and real. My faith had never been tested like this before. I was clearly undone. I didn't know how to trust God this deeply, but I was desperate to be caught and held in what felt like a free fall of out-of-control circumstances.

When I agreed with God that He had the right to orchestrate the events of my life, release replaced the panic and dread. Fear dissolved in the face of my decision to trust God's plan. The intensity of the situation still lingered, but the sense of despair melted away. God anchored my soul and brought me hope. Hope prevailed. Randy and his birth mother survived. After many difficult days, we took our Christmas present home and began to unwrap the gift of him.

I can't explain this defining moment in my faith journey any other way than to say that it was my Damascus Road experience. I understood the truth of 2 Corinthians 12:9 which until that moment had been foreign to me. "My grace is sufficient for you; My strength is made perfect in weakness." I had grown up hearing sermons about that verse, singing songs about it, and I had even won awards for memorizing it. Yet God had determined from eternity past that this night would be the moment He would penetrate my heart with the truth of this verse using laser beam sharpness and unmistakable clarity.

I grasped in a way I never had before what it was like to be cared for by Almighty God in the midst of the storms of *my* life. I was no longer on the sidelines watching someone else. This was *me* … thrust onto center stage. I was terrified. I felt so vulnerable. I didn't recognize or understand it at the time, but God's initiative in letting me know that my heart really mattered to Him somehow propelled me through the many unexpected and demanding days that would lie ahead.

Within weeks after we brought Randy home, Walter and I had made plans to move about eight hours away to complete his internship requirements as a pastor. It was while we were there that I experienced the "desert" of my faith journey, and I began to wonder if I could really stand any more. Hours away from family and friends, it felt like our lives were unraveling. Randy was diagnosed with Cerebral Palsy at 6 months of age. Within a 12-month period, five of my loved ones died or were killed in car accidents, including a special uncle, a dear family friend, an aunt, and my paternal grandma. However, the most difficult was the death of my dad at the age of 56. As I grieved the loss of him, I grieved the loss of Randy's grandpa. He would never get to play ball with him, tell him stories, attend his graduation, or meet any future siblings. I wondered why God would take all that away from us. I also knew that my life would never be the same, as our family dynamics would change in Dad's absence. I enjoyed a unique connection with my dad, one characterized by mutual respect and understanding. He *got me*. He had time for me. I always felt loved, not handled or tolerated. He has been gone for more than 20 years now, but sometimes the ache in my soul to hear him say, "how's my girl?" increases instead of diminishes.

Despite all the difficulty and sorrow in our lives at that time, I was mindful of the fact that I was a "pastor's wife" and with that came both self-imposed and external expectations of godliness. While I did the right things on the outside, my heart was empty, dry, and full of pain. I was the Sunday School superintendent, took my turn as pianist for the worship team, and worked a couple of days a week to help keep the financial bases covered. All during this time, Randy hardly slept for more than an hour or two at a time.

We later learned that he also suffered from asthma. That combined with the low muscle tone in his trunk meant that he would stop breathing, so he would wake up screaming just to catch his breath. I longed for someone to come over so I could sleep more than a couple of hours without interruption.

As is often the case, the biggest struggles in life are not apparent on the outside. That was true of our situation at the church where we were serving. After Walter's internship was complete, the decision was made to hire him in a permanent position. I had prayed before we moved that this ministry experience would be a positive one, not necessarily always easy, but one that would not discourage us from full-time ministry. However, that's not how things played out. We learned, after the fact that Walter was coming in on the heels of a messy situation with the previous youth pastor. As a result, Walter paid a terrible price. Some of the deacons were relentless in their attack on his personality and ministry style. I dreaded every deacon's meeting or invitation he would receive from board members to go out for coffee. While the senior pastor sympathized and supported Walter, he was unable to affect change with the deacons. There was no safe place to share the load in our hearts, so we carried it alone. When we drove out of that city the day we moved, it felt like the death of a dream. The dream of full-time ministry. I had given my heart to the Lord for full-time ministry back in Bible College. Now it seemed like I had been gypped. All the preparation and all that work for only two and a half years of full-time ministry.

We were physically, emotionally, and spiritually depleted. We moved home to my mom's house for the summer until we could secure a place of our own in a city located three hours from where our families lived. This city was a place where intense treatment options with promising results were available for our son. There was an economic boom, housing was hard to find, but the therapy available was one-of-a-kind. We knew we had to make the move. I was so looking forward to being at my mom's house for some down time to recuperate and heal. However, that was not to be. Shortly after we arrived at my mom's, my brother's marriage fell apart. He and his three preschool boys moved in with my mom as well. It was not a time for rest and healing. There was much chaos, and meal times were hectic with four adults and four high chairs seated around the table. My brother's needs were obvious (the care of his three precious boys) and as many of our hurts were internal, they were not evident. We continued to do what we had always done. We carried our pain alone.

Desert Storm

As a result of carrying the load on my own and actually believing that I was *doing* the right thing, my health paid a huge price. I was diagnosed with Rheumatoid Arthritis in October of 2000. The disease was aggressive, and by Christmas of 2000, I was unable to walk by myself if I got too tired. Walter had to cut my meat and help me get dressed. For 3 months, I was unable to care for Randy. This was the same disease that had claimed my dad's quality of life for many years. I knew how much he had suffered. It was daunting to think about what my future could look like. I initially prayed, like Paul, that God would remove this thorn in my flesh, but I've since learned to embrace it as God's uniquely built-in barometer to temper my pace of life.

Within a few months, we were able to find a place and access the intensive therapy for our son. I had undergone a successful drug trial with new medication to address my disease, and we were looking into adopting another child. This adoption ended up being another very painful process in which we were introduced to a child and began to give our hearts to her, only to find out that she wasn't eligible for adoption. Our hearts were tired. We were ready to give up. At a time when we thought our hearts couldn't take any more, another gift arrived for Christmas 2003. The precious little girl who would become our daughter entered our home at age 4. She was like joy in a bottle. Her light-hearted manner and care-free approach to life was a proverbial breath of fresh air that pushed back the heaviness that had threatened to take over our hearts. Her life's journey would prove to be one of further testing and stretching of our faith. The following summer, after becoming our 'keeping kid', our precious little Autumn, began medical testing to address issues that had surfaced as a result of her birth mother's lifestyle choices. By God's grace and Autumn's perseverance, she continues to reflect the beauty and power of the Lord as she daily overcomes the challenges she faces.

We had been attending a seeker-focused church, watching people come to Christ on a regular basis and lapping up the community we were experiencing in our small group. I was invited to join the staff as Office Manager. For the most part I loved the fast-paced life and ministry challenges that came my way. However, the ministry challenge I did not enjoy was the leadership vacuum that surfaced when the founding and senior pastor accepted a call to another church. It was a painful time for the staff, and I learned that leadership is not for the warm and the willing but rather for the gifted and called.

The leadership vacuum was not limited to our church; it was also in our home. The realities of Walter's job meant that he was gone most of the time, and I lived in a state of perpetual exhaustion as I tried to meet the needs of two special-needs kids, serve in a full-time ministry position, and keep things running smoothly in our home. Walter was not only gone physically, he was gone emotionally. I felt the distance between us even when he was home. That was also the time when there was a season of significant strain in my relationship with my mom. This was new to me, and it left me feeling emotionally and spiritually taxed trying to figure out how to honor God, honor her, and maintain my own sanity.

I was starting to feel the effects of the residue left on my heart by repeated disappointments and heartaches. Through all these happenings, I experienced disillusionment at levels I had never known before and a loneliness of soul that I struggled to articulate. I floundered around, not really recognizing that what I wanted most was a soft spot for my heart to land. When I finally realized that was what I was looking for, I also came to the painful realization that some of my greatest assets were also the cause of my greatest pain. I had prided myself in being strong, independent, and efficient. And now I had to admit to myself that those often-admirable traits had allowed me to efficiently use my independence to create my own isolation booth. For the first time, I began to understand that any strength carried to an extreme becomes a weakness.

I now needed people in my life to be for me something that I had not been for them – available. I needed people to just listen and give me perspective. My faith had remained intact, but I needed someone with skin on to remind me of what had fallen off my radar screen in the midst of the struggle.

Streams in The Desert

God knew our souls were drought-weary so He gently guided us to a much-needed oasis. We moved to an acreage (with a creek running through it) and to a church that was much closer to where were living and much larger than the one we had been attending. We arrived *empty* on so many levels and enjoyed the anonymity the large church environment afforded us. We had nothing left to give so we happily faded into the woodwork and soaked up all we could. We had originally thought we had selected that church for Randy's sake because of the vibrant special-needs program it offered. However, God's heart was not just for Randy. He knew what the rest of needed, as well. We needed time to heal. Part of my healing process included attending a women's program they offered on Thursday mornings. There I met other godly women who loved God and lived authentically. It was as the result of one of those friendships that my well-kept secret dream of being a writer and a speaker was brought out of hiding and given wings.

As I entered a class being taught by one of those godly women, I noticed she was teaching material she had written herself. As she handed us three ring binders filled with class notes and 'fill in the blank' guides, I remember thinking, *I could do this.* The class (and now her book) was called *A Woman and Her Relationships.*[7] Attending her class was the beginning of our ever-expanding and deepening relationship. We have taught, traveled and led together many times through the years. Meeting her was clearly a God ordained moment in my life and an answer to my soul's longing for a heart level connection.

That taste of spiritual friendship has been followed up by many more, some with women that have become dear to me. To say I am grateful for their input and impact in my life is inadequate. God has used them immensely to bring healing and shape to my life.

It was a risk for me to reach out to people and actually ask for help. Yet it was worth the risk. I needed to admit to myself and others that I was struggling. I needed to receive the love and care they offered. Finding people who actually cared about me and my heart--not only about the outward, routine happenings of my life—was like experiencing young love again. I felt more energized and alive knowing that others really cared about me. Knowing that the *real me* mattered to others has also significantly changed my outlook on life. Some of the harshness and hardness that characterized my bottom line mentality has been replaced with increasing measures of tenderness and compassion. Not only that, God regularly uses these women to both challenge and encourage me in my walk with Him. When I began to understand the depth of what it means to live in community, it also changed my perspective on neediness. I no longer see godly spiritual friendships as negotiable or *an extra*. They are essential to living a full and authentic life.

There is a freedom that comes from living a life that is authentically me. I have lived, loved, and learned the value of sharing my life with others and letting them build into me. My life is richer, fuller, and a whole lot more fun! I marvel at how God has turned my heart towards spiritual friendship and women's ministry. *Who would have thought?* I've moved from being impatient and annoyed with my gender to having a passionate desire for them to understand that their hearts matter. Only God. Only God could make that kind of transformation.

I titled this section "Streams in the Desert" because God's goodness was flowing into my life in spite of some ongoing desert experiences. I served as an executive assistant to a board of Christian leaders. While I learned much from those seated around the board table, I also got a glimpse into the humanity that plagues us all. About a year after I started serving in that role, Walter decided to start his own business, an RV rental company, of which I was only to be a small part. That's not how things worked out. I ended up resigning my position with the board to keep up with the demands of the business. Being in business is not for the faint of heart, but it made my heart faint on numerous occasions. It also wreaked significant havoc on our marriage. But for the grace of God, we would be in a very bad place. God used my involvement with the business to teach me much about myself. It was an anvil on which He has done some of His deepest work. When you are as task oriented and tenacious as I am, God needs to go to great lengths to bring you to the end of yourself. When He does, you are at a significant crossroads. I floundered for some time, drowning in the waves that blanketed my overwhelmed heart and mind. I was regularly mad, sad, exhausted, and numb as I lived in the chaos of life's demands. I knew that there had to be a better way to live, but I didn't know how to get there.

Streams of Living Water

Lamentations 3:22 says, "Because of the Lord's great love we are not consumed, for His compassions never fail; His mercies are new every morning" (NIV). After what seems like a very long lament, it is with confident assurance and praise that I can say, "Great is His faithfulness." Indeed, life is hard, and God is good, but you don't know how good God can be until you know how hard life can get. Faith learned in the night season has produced a harvest of rich blessing in my life.

God has answered my prayers (and those of others) to turn my heart back to Walter. We are now enjoying a quality of relationship that seemed out of reach not all that long ago. God has granted me the grace to see that my mom was not intentionally trying to hurt me. Her love for me is deep and sincere. We still have different perspectives on that difficult season, but we're both so glad it's over. I still grieve the loss of the closeness my brother and I once had. I continue to pray that it may one day be restored.

I am enjoying ever deepening spiritual friendships. God has shifted my focus, so it is less on tasks and more on people. I am increasingly asking Him to burn His agenda in me rather than blessing my plans. I am enjoying ministry opportunities that nourish my soul and lift my spirit. I have come to the understanding that just as those raised outside the church are uniquely qualified to reach those still outside the faith, God has uniquely prepared me to reach those still lost in the culture of the church, who have a "form of godliness but are denying its power" (2 Timothy 3:5 NKJV). That understanding does not exempt me from reaching out to the lost, but it does anchor my soul and provide clarity and validation for my seat at the kingdom work table. Not to mention providing a strong defense against the "accuser of the brethren" when the battle for my mind rages.

While I am definitely on an upswing on my faith journey, my (and my family's) ongoing successes and struggles keep my feet on the ground. My family provides me with an enduring dose of reality, as they are regularly the recipients of the fallout between who I am and who I want to be. The journey of transitioning Randy out of our home and into a support home brought me to new levels of depletion, but also to a soul-anchoring awareness of God's power, presence, and provision in my life.

I take encouragement and instruction from Peter's second letter to the early church. Peter, who walked with the Lord from the beginning, and *knew* him, still ran ahead of the Lord and missed His promptings and miserably failed Him. Even so, Peter repented, *chose* to receive grace, and went on to be the rock upon which God built His church.

While I'm not happy about everything that has happened in my life, or proud of some of my reactions, I am deeply grateful for God's relentless pursuit of my heart. In the words of Joseph from Genesis 50:20, "what you intended for evil, God intended for good."

Key Learnings:

- ❤ Christ's model was to answer the happenings of life with Scripture.
- ❤ Life is hard, and God is good but you don't know how good God can be until you know how hard life can get.
- ❤ Godly friendships are not negotiable or an extra. They are essential to living a full and authentic life.
- ❤ God never desired for us to live like a pharisee whose heart is dry and empty; He has made a better way to live.
- ❤ Writing our life story is often the first step to finding healing for our hearts.

Questions to Consider:

1. Have you ever written your personal life story? If not, would you be willing to?

2. How have you seen God's goodness in the midst of the hardness of your life?

3. Knowing that answering life with Scripture is the model Christ gave us, what Scripture passages do you need to lean into/memorize?

4. Have you considered praying Scripture into the details of your day?

5. Who might God be asking you to consider engaging in a godly spiritual friendship? (If no one comes to mind, would you commit to making it a regular matter of prayer?)

Passages to Ponder:

"From the end of the earth I will cry to You. When my heart is overwhelmed; Lead me to the rock that is higher than I" (Psalm 61:2 NKJV).

"But those who trust in the LORD will find new strength. They will soar high on wings like eagles. They will run and not grow weary. They will walk and not faint" (Isaiah 40:31).

Prayer of Invitation:

Father God,
As I consider the highs and lows of my life story, I invite the Holy Spirit into my processing. Guide my thoughts and my emotions as I unpack the happenings of my life. Grant me the grace to see beyond the pain to Your relentless pursuit of my heart. Thank You that nothing is outside Your ability to redeem, restore, and renew. Plant seeds of hope within my heart, and let me water them with the truth of Your Word, the fellowship of godly people, and time spent in Your presence. In the strong and powerful name of Jesus, Amen.

Practice Point:

Take some time to write the key elements of your own story. If you're not able to write it all in long form, consider recording it on your smart phone, noting the significant highlights and lowlights that help you chronicle your faith journey. As you do, be mindful of their impact on your heart.

Chapter Three

The Stony Heart: Moving From Wounded to Broken

God doesn't waste our pain ... only we can do that. No doubt, you've had some tragic or heart wrenching experiences of your own. Yet, the happenings of our lives are not unexpected, unnoticed, or unredeemable by God. As stated earlier, they are part of His divine design as He relentlessly pursues what He wants more than anything else—our hearts. God's relentless pursuit of our hearts will almost always involve pain. Why? Because pain is what gets our attention. Just as diamonds are created by pressure, often the beauty of our hearts is forged in the firestorms of our lives. Over time, the squeezing of our souls will demand a response. Left unattended, a hurting heart will surface at unexpected times and often in unwelcome ways. So, what are we to do?

We need to let our pain push us into the arms of our Savior. God brings healing to our pain when we bring our pain to Him. He promises that "My grace is sufficient for you, for my power is made perfect in weakness" (2 Corinthians 12:9b), but somehow we've convinced ourselves that as mature Christians, we shouldn't let situations bother us or that a more stoic approach to life is a sign of holiness. That's not what Christ modelled for us. He met with

His Father regularly not only to get His marching orders but also to share His heart. One can only imagine the depth of pain He was exposed to during His 33 years here on earth—knowing all that He and His Father had envisioned for mankind and then watching their perfect world become ravaged by sin.

The Psalmists also demonstrate the importance of pouring out our hearts to God, most notably, at the beginning of their psalms. While many may end with a spirit of praise, they start with an authentic sharing of the heart. We read in Psalm 77:1-3, "I cry out to God without holding back. Oh, that God would listen to me! When I was in deep trouble, I searched for the Lord. All night long I pray, with hands lifted toward heaven, pleading. There can be no joy for me until he acts. I think of God, and I moan, overwhelmed with longing for his help." Later, in this passage, the psalmist declares, "O God, your ways are holy. Is there any god as mighty as you? You are the God of miracles and wonders!" (vs 13,14). I believe pouring out his heart was the catalyst to the change in perspective the psalmist experienced. I'm not suggesting that it is healthy to become an emotional basket case. We all have our unique personalities and styles in the way we deal with pain. The point is that we need to *acknowledge* our pain and its effect on our lives. When we take it to our Heavenly Father, He meets us in it and take us to places we can't get to in our own strength.

Pain is like a splinter that needs to be removed – you can't heal while it's still inside. The same is true with our hearts. It may not always be pretty when we realize the ugliness that has festered inside of us as a result of refusing to address the pain that has invaded it. Yet, what comes out of us as pressure is applied to the hurting parts of our lives often reveals how deep and sometimes lodged the 'splinter' really is. The only way to promote healing is to rid ourselves of the root cause and the emotional build up that has accompanied it. It could get messy, but failing to deal with pain poisons our souls.

A brutally honest conversation with God is a good place to begin. He is not offended by our emotions. He created them. "For He understands how weak we are; He knows we are only dust"

(Psalm 103:14). God knows this about us and loves us anyway. We have to admit it to ourselves. Our hearts have experienced real pain but not always real healing. What pain do you need to bring to Jesus so He can begin the healing process in you?

I have always been a very organized person who likes to make plans and accomplish much. Most of what you just read in the previous chapter was not part of my *plan*. It thwarted the course I had charted for my life. As the adage goes, "life is what happens while you're making other plans." This can be true even when you're making God-honoring plans. I had a dream I was passionate about. I had planned to be a pastor's wife in a rural community with four children (two boys and two girls) serving with my husband in a relevant, life-changing ministry. I could see it all: tending a large garden, making pies and jam, having lots of people in our home – young and old, seeing lives transformed by the power of Christ. It all seemed so idyllic. I'd even prepared well for it. I learned the fine art of canning, pie making, and hospitality from my mother and grandmother. I'd completed my Bible College degree, and I had supported my husband while he completed his. We had passion and motivation, and we firmly believed this was the life to which God had called us. The course had been charted; the preparations had been made. Now all we needed to do was to work the plan. The only problem with our well-crafted strategy was that it was still missing a crucial element. God knew we needed more preparation—heart preparation. I honestly thought we had prepared well and by God's grace we felt we had all we needed to be effective servants of His. Desire to honor God. *Check.* Sense of vision. *Check.* Education. *Check.* Variety of work and ministry experience. *Check.* Prayed through plans. *Check.*

However, God knew our heart preparation would not be a onetime lesson but would require an intense and ongoing internal training regime. The kind of training that can only be wrestled out in our souls and then lived out decision by decision in response to the happenings of our lives.

Just as with physical training, there are helpful and harmful ways to engage in the process of moving to a place of better health.

So it is with our heart's response to the pain and strain of life. Interestingly enough, it has to do with our posture. Any qualified fitness trainer will tell you that the position your body is in when you respond to the strain that running, stretching, or weight lifting brings will, over time, either bring about the desired results or injure your body. Two people participating in aerobic activity can appear to be doing the exact same thing, but the subtleties of their posture will determine whether they are strengthening the muscles in their knees and ankles or inflicting damaging and unnecessary pressure. The same is true with our hearts. How we respond to the weight and pain of life is in direct correlation to the posture of our hearts. Depending on its position, we will either be strengthening our spiritual faith/trust muscles or inflicting damaging and unnecessary pressure. Our response will determine the trajectory of our lives. While the words *wounded* and *broken* have often been used interchangeably, lived out, they take us down very different paths. One is the way of wearying woundedness, and the other is the way of blessed brokenness. Let's take a look at each path.

Characteristics of Woundedness

Guarded. When our hearts are guarded, we keep people at a comfortable distance. Much mental and significant emotional energy is spent on always, and only, showing our *shiny* side. The notion of being authentic and letting people see our weaknesses is terrifying. Many of our decisions are consciously and unconsciously fueled by the fear of being exposed.

Suspicious/Paranoid. Rooted in insecurity and low self-esteem, wounded hearts continue to second guess themselves and are suspicious of the thoughts and motives of others. They constantly replay interactions and events in their minds asking the question, *what did he/she mean by that?* They are also more likely to commit what psychologists call the Fundamental Retribution Error. In everyday language, that means you assume the worst in others or blame people's actions or the circumstances of their lives on their personality or disposition rather than considering that there might be other factors contributing to their current response or situation. For example: A person's less-than-ideal-response to your interaction with them may have nothing to do with you, but rather than give them the benefit of the doubt, you make a judgment call that they responded the way they did because they are a jerk, etc.

Fatalistic. I call a fatalistic approach the Eeyore complex. The donkey in A.A. Milne's, "Winnie The Pooh" has a pessimistic view of life. Almost everything is more of a bother than he is willing to put forth. Having been pounded by the pain and pressure of life, a wounded heart sees hope as naïve and optimism as childish.

Bitter. Those with wounded hearts have had their faith shaken. By allowing their heart to turn away (or at least pull back) from God, their faith has been weakened. In the process, they have (often times unknowingly) withdrawn mentally, emotionally, and spiritually. As a result, an emptiness of soul emerges, leaving room for seeds of bitterness to take root.

Easily angered. In his book, *Embracing Brokenness*, Alan Nelson notes that "wounded people feel a constant surge of frustration with others."[8] They have unrealistic standards for themselves and others. It's often a case of "there she blows" when their standards are not met.

Self-centered. For someone with a wounded heart, he or she often feels no one has it as bad as them. His or her hardship story always tops anyone else's hardship story. This person tends to minimize others' pain so he or she can focus on the depths of his or her own.

Walking wounded. In a literal sense, this is true. Alan Nelson proposes that there are physical ramifications for people who have not let their circumstances "bring them to a realization of their deep need for God. Psychosomatic and stress induced illnesses are often signs of being broken in the wrong places."[9]

No evidence of the fruit of the Spirit. It's a lot like the plastic fruit you see as part of a display in a restaurant. It looks shiny and even tempting from a distance but has absolutely no nutritional value. That's the state of a wounded person's heart. While he or she knows intellectually of the fruit of the spirit, it is not a part of his or her life-in-the-trenches reality. The life-giving power of the Holy Spirit has been replaced by a flood of self-imposed and self-powered *shoulds* and *ought tos*. They believe they know what a Spirit-filled life should look like and how they ought to act, so they try to fabricate that kind of life. Scripture aptly describes this farce as "having a form of godliness but denying its power" (2 Timothy 3:5).

Relying on self-sufficiency. Believing that God really can't be completely trusted after all, especially in the details of our lives, a wounded heart adopts a mentality that is reflected in many of the mottos common in our world today.

"God helps those who help themselves"

"If it's going to be, it's up to me"

"Every man for himself".

Probably nowhere is this attitude better masked and misunderstood than in church culture. Well-meaning, God-fearing people have bought into the lie that immersing themselves in service will dull the ache in their hearts, so they continue striving in exasperated independence. This approach only fosters further disappointment and creates a bigger pot for disillusionment to stew in.

Harsh. Rooted in impatience and exasperation at not being able to have the life they had hoped for, the words of a wounded heart are often characterized by insensitivity, condescension, and criticism. Once again, scripture reveals its understanding of the human condition, "out of the abundance of the heart the mouth speaks" (Luke 6:45).

If you recognize yourself in any of the characteristics listed above, I want to applaud you for your honesty. More often than I wish were true, some of them have been close companions of mine. We waste our pain when we choose to live in woundedness Notice I said, we waste our pain when we live in woundedness. Remember, God doesn't waste our pain ... only we can do that. There *is* better way to live. Christ modeled it in His life and provided for it through His death.

Understanding Brokenness

Before we proceed any further, I want to make sure we have an accurate understanding of the kind of brokenness I'm referring to. We talk about living in a broken world, with broken lives and broken relationships with sin as the source of the fracture at the core of our being. This fracture separates us from God, from people, and from an accurate understanding of ourselves. In that regard, yes, we are all broken. For the purposes of our discussion, I would like to unpack another way of thinking about brokenness. The kind of brokenness I'm referring to is akin to the taming of a wild horse. A horse is considered "broke" when it surrenders to the governance of its master. It is a difficult progression to take an unruly, scared, and distrusting animal of considerable strength and resolve to a place where it longs to be with and enjoy its new-found owner. However, once that bond is established, there is a calm, welcoming tenderness that replaces the rebellion and skittish fear that once characterized the horse's demeanor. Whether running wild with stubborn independence, grazing on spiritual malaise, or at times bolting in blatant rebellion, our souls also need to be tamed. Admittedly, our hearts are not always intentionally bent on revolt against God, but neither are they naturally bowing in submission to Him. Often, it's a matter of personal pride that needs to be "broke" in our lives. We believe we know best for our lives. When God has other plans, we respond in ways that reflect our selfishness instead of our surrender.

It's important to note that after a horse has been broke, many (not all) of its activities are still the same as they were before—eating, running, working, raising offspring, etc, but the way in which the horse goes about daily activities and the purpose behind them has radically shifted. His posture is no longer one of unbridled defiance but one of stately strength. It now, by the horse's choosing, lives under the protective care of his master.

I'm sure you can see the correlation for our spiritual lives. When it comes to engaging in and enjoying the bond Almighty God desires to have with us, it requires a brokenness that involves submission and yieldedness to God's will and ways. A kind of brokenness that allows a person to recognize their sin and the need for God in order to live the life Christ died to provide. Brokenness is not operated with an on/off switch. It is a work of God that He does in our soul, often without us being cognizant of the process. Only as we look back in reflection can we see the taming He's done in our hearts.

Characteristics of Brokenness

Vulnerable. When our hearts are vulnerable, it's not that we are in a state of weakness as our culture perceives weakness. Rather, we are authentic about who we are and how we feel, both with God and with others. As a result, we are able to give and receive love—again, both from God and from others. James demonstrates the connection between vulnerability and our overall health when he encourages us in James 5:16 to "confess your sins to each other and pray for each other so that you may be healed."

Trusting. Operating from a place of blessed brokenness allows you to believe the best in others. When your motives are pure, it's easier to believe that others' are too. Doing so goes a long way in bringing out the best in others and leaves little room for competition and insecurity.

Optimistic. A heart that has experienced genuine brokenness is anchored in hope. Not a "I really wish" kind of hope, but a confident and grateful sense of expectancy at what God will accomplish through the power of the Holy Spirit.

Better. Better is not a state of denial. Rather, those living from a place of blessed brokenness experience a relationship with God that is deeper and a faith that is stronger. They've learned to lean into God. It's not a case of denying their reality. Instead, it's looking to a greater reality that has the power and grace to change and sustain despite their circumstances.

Even tempered. The refining work of brokenness allows you to set realistic standards for yourself and others. It also grants you the capacity to extend and receive grace to yourself and those around you.

Other centered. A heart honed by brokenness is able to take the focus off of self and find perspective in light of others' situations. Seeing and hearing what God is up to in other people's lives helps expand our view of God's magnitude and sovereignty.

Walking well. People who walk well have brought their pain to Jesus, declared their dependency on Him, and received His ongoing healing in their lives.

Evidence of the fruit of the Spirit. There is nothing plastic about a heart transformed by brokenness. A broken heart exhibits genuine, unexplained peace, contentment, faith, love, and joy, followed closely by patience, kindness, goodness, gentleness, and self-control as produced by the Spirit. None of these are self-effort. See Galatians 5:22.

Resting in God-sufficiency. Those who choose to embrace brokenness declare their dependency on God. They believe to their core that what God calls them to, He will provide the power for. Their confidence in God's sovereignty anchors their soul and releases them from the suffocating weight of *making it happen*. In other words, where God calls, His power falls.

Tender. Tenderness is probably the most distinguishing mark of a heart renovated by brokenness. After being seared in the Refiner's fire and then marinated in the power of God's Word and

His presence, a welcoming and compassionate spirit emerges. One that is sensitive to the heart of the Father and the promptings of the Holy Spirit. Our heart becomes increasingly sensitive to those around us that are caught up in the messiness of life.

You may be thinking to yourself, *you don't know what I've been through*, and you're right. I don't, and I certainly don't want to minimize anyone's pain. However, Scripture uses definitive language when it says "**nothing** is impossible with God" (Mark 10:27 [Emphasis Mine]). "**All** things work together for good ..."(Romans 8:28 [Emphasis Mine]). "Cast **all** your anxiety on Him because He cares for you." (1 Peter 5:7 NIV) [Emphasis Mine].

When our heart is hurting deeply, passages like this can seem hollow, empty, and almost insensitive. Yet, how we feel about a particular verse does not determine whether or not it's true. God's character and His Word are the real measures of truth. Both are unchanging, and neither is bound by human emotion or cultural relativism. But neither God nor His Word are cold and unfeeling. Just the opposite. "The Lord is like a father to his children, tender and compassionate to those who fear him" (Psalm 103:13). As a demonstration of His love and compassion for us, He provided His Word as an anchor for us to hold onto no matter where our emotions may be flinging us. (Having been raised on a farm, the analogy of a fly on a cow's tail comes to mind.)

Still the question remains: How do I move from woundedness to brokenness? In response to that question, I am going to share with you a statement that I am likely to repeat a few times in the pages ahead. "If it was easy, more people would do it and do it well." Or as Ann Spangler puts it,

> "Spiritual growth is difficult and it's often counterintuitive. Jesus tells me to stop worrying, yet my sleepless nights persist. He tells me to turn the other cheek when my instinct is to raise the other fist. He talks of dying and carrying a cross when all I want to do is enjoy every minute of the life I have...I can't get it through my head

that there's no such thing as an easy path for becoming the person Christ calls me to be."[10]

Moving from Woundedness to Brokenness

Changing starts with an act of our will. While God deeply desires for us to embrace brokenness rather than living as the walking wounded, He will not force us. The choice is ours. He eagerly and graciously extends the invitation but waits for us to respond to His leadings and promptings. The decision lies completely within our control. Lest you become discouraged at this point, please consider your options. (And God's kindness!) God's Word tells us there is a better way to live—a life characterized by uncommon peace, unearned grace, and unexpected joy. We can either move toward trusting God and His Word and choose to submit to His will and ways, (we can always ask for His help, even in this) or we can continue to try and cope with our chaos. While we may try to suggest (or even create) other options, the bottom line is, there are only two.

I would propose that for all of us, it's a case of *when we've been in the desert long enough, we'll do whatever it takes to get out*. I was probably in the desert for a considerable amount of time before I even realized I was there. I thought I was handling my situation pretty well until the parched places in my heart began to surface and a splash of religious activity could no longer hydrate the intense dryness I felt in my soul.

Once I realized I was in a desert, I also realized I had no clue how to get out of it. As my exasperation grew, my hope dwindled. I remember feeling completely overwhelmed and saying to God, "Really, is this as good as it gets? I thought following You would look and feel different than this." At first, I felt guilty for even thinking or saying those words, but in the midst of my desperation to feel joy again, I became very honest with God, especially concerning how I felt about my life and His seeming unwillingness to help me in my struggles. Those raw conversations started a journey that continues today—my ongoing journey from woundedness to brokenness.

Throughout the remaining chapters, we will unpack more of the specifics of what moving from woundedness to brokenness looks like, but for now I would like to suggest three fundamental and overarching principles that will serve as pillars to support us in that journey from woundedness to brokenness.

EAT

Embrace the process.

Ask God for What You Need.

Trust Him.

Embrace the process

Once, while serving on a church staff, I had a colleague challenge me to embrace my current life situation. I said, "I don't know how." In my exasperation, I wanted someone to tell me what to do. I've since learned that embracing a situation or process is more an attitude than it is an action. Rather than resisting it or wishing circumstances away, I can invite God to use those circumstances to accomplish their intended purposes. Instead of attempting to regain control by trying to change circumstances or people, I have the option to choose a teachable spirit and learn from God and others.

Lest you think I have mastered this principle, please let me share a word of caution born out of my own failings. When we embrace the process, we have to do so for what the process itself will accomplish in us, not for the end product. Guaranteed, God's redemptive and refining processes in your life will take longer than you have patience for. We short circuit God's honing work in our lives when we attempt to force His agenda by trying in our own strength to learn the lesson faster or take a more direct route to where we think He wants us to be. For someone who values efficiency as much as I do, it's tempting to endeavor to discern what lesson God is trying to teach me and then try to expedite the process. *After all, that should bring a more expedient end to the discomfort I'm feeling and besides, wouldn't God be pleased with my desire to become more like Him as quickly as I can?*

The irony and great error in that line of thinking is that my actions demonstrate I have an even harder and quite likely much longer lesson to learn. The timing and length of the process are God's decisions, not mine. God is a supernatural God, and so are His ways. (Isaiah 55:11) We won't always be able to understand or explain the method or the timing of the change and perspective He brings to our hearts. Gratefully, we don't have to. While God reveals much of Himself in His Word, 1 Corinthians 13:12 reminds us, "For now we see only a reflection as in a mirror; then we shall see face to face. Now I know in part; then I shall know fully, even as I am fully known" (NIV). God knows every intricacy of our lives. Yet we are ill equipped to fully comprehend His sovereignty. So we get to choose—resist the sovereignty of our God, (Who is for us), or embrace it.

Ask God for What You Need

"You do not have because you do not ask God" (James 4:2 NIV). "*Only ask*, and I will give you the nations as your inheritance, the whole earth as your possession" (Psalm 2:8 NLT [Emphasis Mine]). I believe we sometimes extend our seasons of pain because we don't ask God for His help, especially *in the moment*. I didn't used to talk out loud to God very much when I was by myself, but through the years, as depletion and desperation tumbled out of my heart and into my mouth, I would often hear myself saying, "God, where are You? Won't You please help me?" I can't begin to tell you how many times God came. He came! *And* brought His grace to bear on my situation. My faith truly came alive when I invited God into my moments and experienced His grace. Stormie Omartian defines God's grace as "Divine assistance that is undeserved."[11] We all agree on our need for God's grace, but how often do we forget to ask for it, especially in the middle of the firestorms of our lives? When we try to find solutions on our own, we can become disillusioned with God, frustrated that He didn't come through for us. Not only that, life becomes like a *whac a mole* game, constantly pushing down our pain even though it keeps popping up (it might be fun at first, but soon it gets exhausting).

God will not force His way into our lives, nor is He a helicopter parent that dives in to rescue us from any and all discomfort. He is a loving Heavenly Father who tells us that the help we're looking for comes from "casting all your cares on Him because He cares for you" (1 Peter 5:7 HCSB). If we actually understood *how much* He cares for us, we would invite His divine assistance into every part of our day—not just the hard parts. God clearly wants us to ask for His help, but the Psalmist reminds us, "When I consider your heavens, the work of your fingers, the moon and the stars, which you have set in place, what is mankind that you are mindful of them, human beings that you care for them?" (Psalm 8:3,4). I trust you can see how ludicrous it is to be demanding of the Creator of the universe. No matter the depth of our pain, the posture of our heart needs to be that of one that is receiving "divine assistance that is *undeserved.*"

Trust Him

These two words, "Trust Him" are so much easier to read, write, and say than they are to live out. However, making the decision to trust God's character and His Word in the midst of the depth of our pain develops the faith muscles that are at the core of living with our hearts at rest. Reaching out in faith and asking for God's grace to sustain us gives us what we need to persevere. If you're in the middle of a dark and difficult season, these words may ring hollow. Yet it's in times like these that our hearts need to counsel our minds to trust even though we don't understand. For it is in times like these that our faith becomes very meaningful or it means nothing at all! Only when our heads and our hearts work in tandem will we enjoy the soul-anchoring rest that our spirits crave. Psalm 62:5 tells us that "I find rest in God; only he gives me hope" (NCV), and Isaiah 26:3 promises, "You will keep in perfect peace all who trust in you, all whose thoughts are fixed on you!" (NLT).

You will notice that the first letter of each of these principles form the acronym EAT. Just as eating is essential to our physical existence, I believe these concepts are at the core of our spiritual vitality and inextricably linked to our soul's rest. Our faith is not based on our feelings but on our choice to believe God and His Word. If you're struggling with these concepts, I encourage you to stick with it. We'll unpack more of the questions and objections your heart may be feeling right now in the next chapter.

Key Learnings:

- Over time, the squeezing of our souls *will* demand a response.
- Pain is like a splinter – you can't heal while it's still inside.
- The posture of our heart determines our response to pain. Will it be woundedness or brokenness?
- God doesn't waste our pain ... only we can do that.
- Our faith comes alive when we ask God in the moment to bring His grace (Divine assistance) to bear on our situation.
- Our faith is not based on our feelings.

Questions to Consider:

1.   What pain do you need to bring to Jesus so He can begin the healing process in you?

2.   In what ways have you learned to cope with your chaos?

3.   Is your life characterized by woundedness or brokenness? What needs to change? Be specific.

4.   What scares you most about embracing brokenness?

5.   How might the EAT acronym make a difference in how you respond to pain and difficulty in your life?

Passages to Ponder:

"Pour out your hearts like water to the Lord. Lift up your hands to him in prayer" (Lamentations 2:19).

"My grace is sufficient for you, for my power is made perfect in weakness" (2 Corinthians12:9b).

Prayer of Invitation:

Lord God,
Thank You for the life You died to provide for me. Help me desire to move from woundedness to brokenness. Anchor my soul, steady my heart, and focus my mind. Strengthen my hand when it feels too weak to reach up and grasp Yours. Develop a posture of humility in my heart and prepare it for the unexpected joy You desire to bring.

Practice Point:

Spend some time pouring out your pain to God. Grant God access to remove the splinters in your heart. Go for a long walk. Talk to God or journal. Lay on your bed sobbing - whatever way helps you to open up your heart. Pouring out our pain *is* painful, but so is holding it all in. The first time is the most difficult as there is so much pressure built up within our hearts. If you've experienced some significant trauma in your life, you may consider seeking out a professional Christian counselor to help you navigate this step.

Think back to the practice point from chapter one. This is where our new spiritual habits feel awkward and foreign. On an ongoing basis, when you are standing in front of the mirror in the morning, look yourself in the eye. Ladies, before you apply your make up, ask yourself, "Is there any pain I'm trying to cover up?" Gentlemen, as you apply your deodorant, ask yourself, "Is there something I'm trying to mask?"

Chapter Four

The Softened Heart: Moving from Pain to Perspective

Pain is the number one reason we live out of our head instead of our heart and it causes us to question what we believe about God and His character. This gap neutralizes our ability to experience all He has designed for us. In this chapter, we will focus on how to better recognize that disconnect in our lives and explore ways to re-engage our hearts.

You recall the analogy between pain and a splinter. Well, as we all know, getting a splinter is not a once in a lifetime thing. Despite our efforts to avoid them, they happen. And when they do, we need to deal with them…again. Sometimes, quite invasively. (ie tweezers, disinfectant or medical intervention) Without good wound care, infection automatically sets in. The same is true of the pain that infects our hearts. Guarding our heart requires that we are consistent in addressing the pain that comes our way throughout life. Just as quick and thorough attention is needed to tend to a splinter, good soul care is required to gain and maintain the perspective necessary for genuine joy. Left unattended, infection spreads and poisons our body. Ignoring our internal pain only multiplies its effects and allows it to become toxic to our souls.

I understood this much more clearly after attending a writer's conference several years ago. While we were there, we were given opportunity to schedule appointments with accomplished writers, publishers, agents, and other professionals. I had scheduled an appointment with Jan Johnson, who has written several books including, *Enjoying the Presence of God* and *When The Soul Listens.* I had great aspirations of talking to her about the project I was working on and gleaning from her author wisdom and experience. That's not how things played out. She started the conversation by asking a little about me, and as I attempted to give her a brief synopsis of my life, I burst into tears. (Like I said in chapter three, left unattended, a hurting heart will surface at unexpected times and often in unwelcome ways.) You need to know that people who know me well would not describe me as squishy or ever given to public displays of emotion. I was shocked. I had shared my story countless times before and really thought I was OK with it all. As we talked, I learned I had not actually dealt with my pain; I had compartmentalized it. More than I realized or wanted to admit, I was still living in woundedness.

Even when we're trying to live in God-honoring brokenness, the larger the gap between our dreams and our reality, the more angst we feel. Over time, as the monotony of life takes its toll, and when we can no longer see any chance of our dreams becoming reality, our natural defense mechanism is to tune out. Sometimes it's conscious, but often it's a subconscious decision to pull back and disengage in an attempt to protect our hearts. As the color in our lives begins to fade to grey, subconscious emotional self-preservation mechanisms take over, not unlike those our material body employs when it senses danger. The physical fight or flight response in us kicks in on instinct, and our emotions do the same. When we no longer have the strength or desire to stand up and fight in the emotional arena of our lives, our tendency is to lose heart and engage the flight response. We exert significant emotional energy to make sure we will not be exposed to that level of hurt again. Basically, *if no one gets in, no one can hurt me.* The depth of our pain is often reflected in the corresponding thickness and intensity with which we craft the walls around our hearts.

Not all of our hurts and disappointments are on a crisis level, but the combined weight of lesser issues can produce overwhelming pressure. Emotionally exhausted and feeling psychologically snowed under, we feel we have no other option but to withdraw ourselves and our hearts from the cold, uncaring world around us. One-by-one, the doors of our heart slam shut as we desperately try to numb the pain of repeated disappointments and unrelenting hurt. May I remind you, that we can only shut off so many parts of our heart until all that is left is a shell. You know people like this; maybe you're one of them. The light has gone out in their eyes, and they are existing through life. They would rather feel nothing than deal with constant pain and inner turmoil. So, they've convinced themselves the only way to make it through life is to live out of their heads and disengage their hearts. They've opted to work with the facts and leave feelings out of the matter.

It has always been God's divine intention that we would live with our heads and our hearts working in tandem, but in an attempt to keep the internal chaos at bay, many choose to turn off their spiritual and emotional heart valves. Using the analogy of our head and hearts being like a team of two horses working together to pull a heavy load, if one horse is injured and becomes incapacitated, the other horse is then required to shoulder the entire load without the help or momentum of its companion. It's not just about the loss of the injured horse's strength, it's also about the loss of collective momentum that's only possible when the two work together. We lose far more than half of ourselves when we choose to live solely out of our heads.

Sadly, this mentality is just as prevalent among Christians as it is in the rest of the population, perhaps even more so. After all, what good and godly person wants to admit the disillusionment, disappointment, or flat-out anger they feel toward God and what He's allowed to happen in their life? Yet, if we're honest enough to admit it, we often feel anger when faced with overwhelming circumstances. And like Adam and Eve, we try to hide ourselves and our feelings from God. We are deceived into thinking it is wrong to have or express our emotions and that doing so will be an offense. We fear the consequences. That mindset couldn't be farther from the truth. By divine design, God put the capacity to experience the *whole* gamut of emotions that He *created* in each one of us. He knew that we would need them to experience and express the totality of what life in our world would bring. Allowing emotions as part of our human experience contributes significantly to our physical, mental, and spiritual wholeness.

Emotions are also necessary as we explore the one question that is fundamental to moving forward from a place of pain to soul anchoring perspective. The question before each of us when our hearts are gripped by pain is this: "Is God Good? Really?" You may have been expecting a deeper or more theologically framed question, but the reality is, your answer to this simple question has implications that span the highest of highs and lowest of lows in all of your life. Your response, whether you believe God is always good, becomes the foundation that determines your capacity to trust God and His Word. When your head and heart believe God's Word and that His character is forever trustworthy, they become twin anchors for living with your heart at rest.

His heart is for us, even when we can't see His hand at work. Out of the depth of His love for us, He is there to help us, even when we doubt Him and His character. As we wrestle our way through trouble to a place of trust, He promises, "I will never fail you. I will never abandon you" (Hebrews 13:5). Learning to trust God can be scary because we don't always see our lives through the lens of His perspective or His power. Please remember, you can't be brave unless you're scared first.

Bravery, by its own nature requires action in the presence of fear. Action in the absence of fear is nothing more than daily living. Living lives empowered by the Holy Spirit allows fear to serve as a catalyst for bravery. We would have reason to be scared (and deeply discouraged) if we were left to our own devices to create the rest our souls need. Take heart and great encouragement from the fact that you can't create it. For when you truly understand that you can't get to a place of deep soul rest on your own, you are then in a place to receive God's grace (divine assistance) which fills that unrelenting longing in our hearts. I trust that as we continue to grapple with this issue, looking through the lens of Scripture, you will come to see God's essence of goodness and why He is worth trusting with all our hearts.

Precious few things in life are as easy as ABC, and learning to trust God certainly isn't one of them. However, these letters provide the abbreviation for three guiding principles I believe will help focus our hearts and minds on our journey to fully trusting God.

A—Agree with the Almighty.

He has the right to orchestrate the events of your life.

A is where the alphabet begins and this first step is where the journey to a heart at rest also begins. You won't be able to move out of where you are until this foundation of agreeing with the Almighty is in place in your life.

We all agree it is good to trust God, but do we trust Him? For those of us who know Christ as our personal Savior, we have entrusted our *eternity* to Him, but what about this life here and now? Do we trust God with the happenings of our day to day lives? I believe we think we do, but when the heat is on, we don't behave like we do, causing us to become frustrated at our inability to do better, followed by exasperation at God's seeming disinterest in resolving our difficulties. Trailing close behind comes a level of disillusionment with God that can spiral into guilt, hopelessness, and finally, despair. We get stuck in this cycle, which gives great pleasure to the enemy of our soul.

Barring God's divine intervention, your overall circumstances (your spouse, your children, your job, your relationships, and all the issues that go with them) are unlikely to change, so the only thing you can change is your perspective. If you choose to get mad, discouraged, or otherwise live in woundedness, then you continue spinning on a never ending cycle and nothing happens. Except you become bitter, harsh, and filled with hopelessness. These characteristics are not God's heart for you. There truly is a better way to live.

As God is, so life is. If God is good, life is good; if He's not, then life is an endurance test in misery. How you see God will determine how you see and do life. Scripture offers several core concepts that must frame our view of God.

God is Sovereign

Daniel 4:35 tells us, "He does as He pleases with the powers of heaven and the peoples of earth. No one can hold back His hand or say to Him: What have You done?"

Philippians 2:13 reminds us, "For it is God which worketh in you both to will and to do of his good pleasure" (KJV). You may feel your spirit bristling a little at this thought, thinking of all the ways God's sovereignty hasn't fixed your life. I heard a story that helped bring my churning thoughts into perspective.

A man went to the barbershop to have his hair cut and his beard trimmed. As the barber worked, they began to have a good conversation. They talked about various subjects. When they eventually touched on the subject of God, the barber said, "I don't believe that God exists."

"Why do you say that?" asked the customer.

The barber replied, "Well, you just have to go out in the street to realize that God doesn't exist. Tell me, if God exists, would there be so many sick people?" Would there be abandoned children? If God existed, there would be neither suffering nor pain. I can't imagine a loving God who would allow all of these things."

The customer thought for a moment but didn't respond because he didn't want to start an argument. The barber finished his job, and the customer left the shop.

Just after he left the barbershop, he saw a man in the street with long, stringy, dirty hair and an untrimmed beard. He looked dirty and unkempt. The customer turned back and entered the barber shop again and said to the barber, "You know what? Barbers do not exist."

"How can you say that?" asked the surprised barber. "I am here, and I am a barber. And I just worked on you!"

"No!" the customer exclaimed. "Barbers don't exist because if they did, there would be no people with long, dirty hair and untrimmed beards like that man outside."

"Ah, but barbers DO exist! That's what happens when people do not come to me."

"Exactly!" affirmed the customer. "That's the point! God, too, does exist! That's what happens when people do not go to Him and don't look to Him for help. That's why there is so much pain and suffering in the world."

We can think about this story in the context of world issues, but what about the issues that are impacting our individual world? Are we more like the customer who came to the barber, trusted the barber's expertise and allowed the barber to work on him (remember, barbers use very sharp tools!), or are we more like the unkempt man outside that allowed the harshness of life to diminish his appearance and give people reason to believe (albeit falsely) that barbers don't exist?

Psalm 145:17-19 teaches us that "The LORD is righteous in all his ways and loving toward all he has made. The LORD is near to all who call on him, to all who call on him in truth. He fulfills the desires of those who fear him; he hears their cry and saves them." If God is indeed righteous (good) and loving, can we agree with His decision to allow certain circumstances in our lives that we would not have chosen for ourselves? Submitting to God's sovereignty does not mean that life won't be hard or that we won't hurt. We all know by experience the truth of John 16:33, "in this world you will have trouble." What submitting to God's sovereignty does mean is that we're surrendering the determination of the elements of our life to God. He gets to decide what is and isn't allowed in our lives, and we agree that all His choices are right. Our human nature is not naturally bent toward submission, and doing so requires a conscious uncommon choice on our part. The more we get to know His Word and His character, the more we come to understand the gift God's sovereignty brings to our lives.

God is Merciful, Not Vindictive

Psalm 103:10-12 reads, "He has not punished us for all our sins, nor does He deal with us as we deserve. For His unfailing love toward those who fear Him is as great as the height of the heavens above the earth. He has removed our rebellious acts as far away from us as the east is from the west." While there are consequences for our actions, God is not mean-spirited or malicious. He is not looking for the chance to bring difficulty into our lives. Matthew 7:11 reminds us, "So if you sinful people know how to give good gifts to your children, how much more will your heavenly Father give good gifts to those who ask him."

"Do you show contempt for the riches of his kindness, forbearance and patience, not realizing that God's kindness is intended to lead you to repentance?" (Romans 2:4 NIV).

One of the ways we see God's mercy toward us is in His intense desire and ability to redeem the *slop* of our lives. Growing up (long before composting became popular), we had a bucket that held scraps, peels, and unwanted household liquids. The contents of the bucket was known as *slop* in our kitchen. We tried to empty the bucket or at least put it out of sight when we knew company was coming. I believe that slop bucket is an apt description of the unwanted and sometimes indescribable circumstances in our lives and how we try to manage them. Sometimes our *slop* comes through no fault of our own; other times it is the direct result of our own selfish choices. However your *slop* came to you, God wants to come even closer, draw you to Himself, and make a way where there seems to be no way in those dark and painful parts of your life. Joel 2:25 describes it as "restoring the years the locusts have taken."

Satan would have us believe that if we're suffering from poor choices we've made, then we've sealed our fate, and there's no way out. While Scripture is clear that there are consequences for sin, may I remind you that beating ourselves up over wrong choices or decisions we've made suggests God's ability to work is limited to our choices. Whether we recognize it or not, that line of thinking suggests that God is not free to act independently of our poor choices. We're actually acting like we can bind up His power.

Certainly, God won't force His way into our lives, but we can't contain or control the power of Almighty God. If we believe He is all powerful, then why would we think that our decisions would limit His ability to act on our behalf? 2 Chronicles 20:6 reaffirms, "O LORD, God of our ancestors, You alone are the God who is in heaven. You are ruler of all the kingdoms of the earth. You are powerful and mighty; no one can stand against You." Rather than attempting to engage in a power struggle with God (Haven't we all tried and failed?), receive His mercy and embrace His sovereignty that empowers His desire to redeem the *slop* of your life. You will see that like the compost pile, what once was unwanted and even brought a stench to your life can become a source of new life within your soul.

God's Plans Are Not Always Readily Visible

Isaiah 55:8,9 says, "'My thoughts are completely different from yours,'" says the LORD. "'And my ways are far beyond anything you could imagine. For just as the heavens are higher than the earth, so are my ways higher than your ways and my thoughts higher than your thoughts.'" The Message translation reads, "I don't think the way you think. The way you work is not the way I work." Remember that the A stands for Agree with the Almighty. He has the right to orchestrate the events of your life. Notice that there is intention in orchestration. It is not random or haphazard. It carries a sense of deliberate arrangement not unlike a conductor leading an orchestra through a complex piece of music. Psalm 139:13-17 notes God's intentionality in your life, "For you created my inmost being; you knit me together in my mother's womb. I praise you because I am fearfully and wonderfully made; your works are wonderful, I know that full well. My frame was not hidden from you when I was made in the secret place. When I was woven together in the depths of the earth, your eyes saw my unformed body. *All the days ordained for me were written in your book before one of them came to be.* How precious to me are your thoughts, O God! How vast is the sum of them!" [Emphasis Mine].

Ephesians 2:10 reminds us, "For we are God's masterpiece. He has created us anew in Christ Jesus, so that we can do *the good things he planned for us long ago.*" [Emphasis Mine].

Even though we may be surprised by our situation or circumstances, God is not. Do you believe that statement? When you lose your job? When your daughter tells you she's pregnant? When you get the diagnosis? When someone you love hurts you deeply? When the phone rings and you hear the words, "there's been an accident"? When …?

While any of the circumstances listed above may make your heart beat a little faster, not one of them catches God off guard. In fact, James 1:2-4 tells us, "Dear brothers and sisters, whenever trouble comes your way, let it be an opportunity for joy. For when your faith is tested, your endurance has a chance to grow. So, let it grow, for when your endurance is fully developed, you will be strong in character and ready for anything."

If you're like me, there may be times in your life when you think, *God, I believe I've had enough character building for right now. Thank you very much.* The times when you think like that, can be the times when He turns up the heat. In the midst of the struggle, we can become like the passenger on the back of a bicycle built for two forever tapping Jesus on the shoulder, asking "where are we going?" "how much longer?" "are You sure this is the right way?" all to which Jesus turns and lovingly replies, "shut up and peddle." This was an analogy relayed to me by a dear friend many years ago, and it highlights the fact that there will be seasons in our life which we simply don't understand what's happening or how it could be used for our good or His glory. Rather than striving to figure out God's plans, we would do well to simply lean into our Savior and keep peddling. This is not an act of blissful denial but rather one of intentional and joyful dependence.

God is not afraid of your questions. In fact, in James 1:5-6, He invites us to ask, "If you need wisdom—if you want to know what God wants you to do—ask him, and he will gladly tell you.

He will not resent your asking. But when you ask him, be sure that you really expect him to answer" (THE MESSAGE). If we ask, He will answer and this passage reminds us that God does not resent our asking. No, God is not afraid of your questions, in fact, He invites them, but He may just tell you that you're asking the wrong ones! (We want to know "why," and He wants to show us "what," and He wants to teach us "how" whatever we are asking for will make a difference in our lives.)

The life of Joseph recorded in the closing chapters of Genesis is a vivid example of God's plans not being readily visible. Sold into slavery by his brothers, falsely accused of sexual impropriety, disgraced, imprisoned, promised the hope of release and then forgotten. These are not a list I'd like on my resume! Yet God used each of them (over the course of 13 years I might add) to refine him, restore him, and bring him to a place of power, second only to the ruling authority of the entire land. Joseph had plenty of opportunity to waste away in bitterness. All these events happened to him while he was living a God-honoring life. To say there were some significant injustices in his life would be an understatement. Yet in Genesis 50:20, he demonstrates his understanding of the sovereignty and goodness of God when he proclaims to his family, "You intended to harm me, but God intended it all for good. He brought me to this position so I could save the lives of many people" (NIV).

Paul reflects a similar posture of heart in Romans 11:33-36 when he says, "Oh, how great are God's riches and wisdom and knowledge! How impossible it is for us to understand his decisions and his ways! For who can know the LORD's thoughts? Who knows enough to give him advice? And who has given him so much that he needs to pay it back? For everything comes from him and exists by his power and is intended for his glory. All glory to him forever! Amen." God is always up to a thousand more things than the obvious. Trying to figure out God is an exercise in exasperation. Rather than letting your mind's capacity provide the borders for God's wisdom and power, rest in, and enjoy the expanse of His sovereignty.

B – Busy is not Better

We live in a culture where busyness is directly related to importance. Think about it; when someone asks, "How are you doing?" most people respond with, "busy," and then they begin to list all the things they've done, are doing, or plan to do. The longer the list, the more important and impressive they sound, right? It's exhausting. We can get tired simply listening to the cacophony of activity. But the exhaustion isn't only physical, it's also emotional and spiritual.

There's a story about a group of Sherpas (guides/pack carriers) who had been hired by some Western mountain climbers to take them up to the top of Mount Everest. The Westerners had gotten a late start on their trek and were pushing hard each day to make up for it. One morning, after several days of intense hiking and climbing, the Sherpas refused to move. No amount of pressure or prodding could get them to budge from the rock they were sitting on. Finally, in exasperation, the men who had employed their services asked, "why can't you move?" They responded by saying, "We can't go any farther. We have to wait for our spirits to catch up with our bodies."

I believe their answer accurately describes the longing in the core of our being that often goes unnoticed or unheeded. The internal revving we sometimes feel may actually be our heart panting to get its breath as it races to catch up with our pace of life. As the saying goes, "If the enemy can't make you bad, he'll make you busy." He knows the effects of depletion on your heart. He is more than happy to have us perpetually exhausted, distracted from what really matters, while we struggle to just keep up with life.

Unfortunately, I know only too well the emptiness of soul that comes from incessant busyness. Raising children with special needs, working outside the home (sometimes full time, sometimes part time), significant involvement in our local church and having a husband who worked away most of the time left me perpetually empty with nothing left to give, especially to my family. Many times as I was rushing from one thing to the next, I would say, "God please fill me, God please fill me. Can't You see this load I'm carrying?" His response was tender but unmistakable, "Sweet pea, it's hard to fill a moving bucket." Similar advice was given to the children of Israel as they found themselves pinned between the raging Egyptians and the mighty Red Sea. As panic began to swell into full-blown terror, "Moses told the people, 'Don't be afraid. Just **stand still** and watch the Lord rescue you today'" (Exodus 14:13 NLT [Emphasis Mine]).

Many of you are aware that Psalm 46:10, *"Be still and know that I am God,"* was written in the context of overwhelming circumstances. In this verse, the Psalmist speaks of God's invitation to an uncommon way of life—a life characterized by surprising calm despite turbulent circumstances. God joyfully offers the rest we're looking for, but it comes to us in ways that are counter-intuitive. In our flesh, we feel compelled to move or be drawn into the chaos when we're in the middle of the firestorms of our lives. God offers a better way.

Solitude and silence seem to be the forgotten disciplines of our faith. Romans 8:16 tells us, "For His Holy Spirit speaks to us deep in our hearts and tells us that we are God's children." That is God's promise to us. *By His Spirit He affirms us as His sons and daughters so we can know in the core of our beings we are known and loved by Almighty God.* A passing glance at that last sentence might make it seem like not a big deal, but I must tell you that it is a huge deal. We all know stories of people who turn themselves inside out trying to win the love and/or affirmation of their earthly father. There is a settledness in those who know they have it and an unsettling striving in those who don't. The same is true spiritually. Often the hurriedness of our lives and the constant drive to do more, be more, have more is rooted in that insatiable desire to be enough for God. One of the identifying marks of someone who is living with their heart at rest is an anchored settledness that characterizes and influences the entire being of someone who knows Who they belong to and how much they are loved. Friends, God longs to speak love and affirmation deep into our hearts, but with nonstop entertainment, endless TV, portable technology, and social media with almost unhindered connectivity combined with an unrelenting schedule, I wonder if we'd ever hear Him? In all the clamor, when we can't hear His voice, we become disheartened, and then we accuse God of not speaking to us.

Regularly throughout Scripture, we see that Christ intentionally got away from people, noise, and distraction to simply be with His Father. As was often taught as I was growing up, Jesus did this to get His marching orders from God the Father. While no doubt this is true, I also believe Jesus needed time to let the Father pour His love and affirmation into Him. After all, He had a lot of difficult circumstances and frustrating people to contend with on a regular basis. His prayers were not one sided. He made time to be still and quiet long enough to hear His Father speak. One thing is clear-both pouring out our hearts to God and letting Him pour into ours are necessary to move us from pain to perspective.

C – Choose to Change

When we are not intentional about choosing change, by default, we are choosing chaos. The chaos of striving and striving and striving to be or do something we believe is necessary to please or appease God, is never His heart for us when He invites us to surrender our lives to Him. Many of us, me included, fear the loss of control. Few things create the level of panic that surfaces when we feel we are losing control. Losing control of our relationships, our health, our sense of security or our dreams, just to name a few. As I was teaching a class on this topic, the Lord prompted me with a thought that has since provided many course corrections in my thinking. It goes like this, *If I have to be in control of everything, then all I can ever have is what I can manufacture and that leaves no room for what God can do.* Read that again, and let it sink into your soul.

Rather than change, many people learn to cope with their chaos. Their rationale might go something like this, *While it may not be pretty, at least it's familiar and I've learned how to manage it... well, sort of.* Scripture has some pretty strong words for that line of thinking, "As a dog returns to its vomit, so a fool repeats his foolishness" (Proverbs 26:11 NLT).

I invite you to consider for a moment how you have learned to cope with your chaos—your internal revving, your anger, your habits, your insecurity, your relationships, your _____. What strategies have you employed to help you manage your chaos?

I remember during a time of "Intense Fellowship" (aka arguing) with my husband, I was expressing my frustration with the magnitude of the load I was carrying, and I let him know that I didn't feel he was helping enough or meeting my needs. I told him how unhappy I was and that much of the blame lay in his lack of physical help and emotional support. As I finished venting, he asked, "Do you even want to be happy?" At first I thought, *of course I do, and if you'd just help me more I could be.* But as I pondered his question, I realized I was taking the easy way out. It was easier to complain and let myself be overwhelmed than it was to take responsibility for my actions and attitudes and then make the necessary changes. I needed to *choose* to be still and let God fill me (before the kids got up) and renew my mind like we read in Romans 12:1,2. I needed to ask Him to help me think about my life the way He wanted me to, not expecting from others what God Himself longed to give me. Rest ... right ... in the middle of the stuff of life. That's what brought the joy back into my life. It came from the work Christ did in my heart from the inside out, not something I pasted on the outside. The transforming power of Christ cannot always be explained or understood. We will talk in future chapters about some specific strategies that you may find helpful, but before any of that will be of value, we must decide, by a deliberate act of our will that by God's grace we in fact do want to change. Beth Moore calls it changing our *want to.*[12] Oh, how many times I have prayed that God would change my want to.

Earlier I mentioned that I came to the realization that even though I thought I had dealt with my pain, I had only compartmentalized it. While that is a common reaction to unwanted pain, unbeknownst to many, (including me) that hidden compartment becomes what fuels the internal revving inside us. No amount of management will keep it from festering. We will not experience significant or sustained change in our perspective until we *decide* to willingly allow God to have His way. As you are pondering the wrestle that you may be feeling in your spirit right now, may I remind you that our lives are like the wake a boat leaves behind once it has passed through the water. Despite our very best efforts to manage our chaos, our lives will leave an indisputable wake that reflects the choices we made in our lifetime. When speaking of our wake, Dr. Henry Cloud in his book, *Integrity*, notes, "It does not lie and doesn't care about excuses."[13]

We are not nesting dolls—you know, the ones that stack inside of each other. We cannot take parts of our inside life out and set them on the shelf without experiencing the resulting hollowness left inside of us. Any of us who have tried know only too well the unresolved angst of, *there's got to be more; what am I missing?* May I also remind you to keep your eyes on the prize—the opportunity to integrate all the compartments of your life into one authentic, healthy, whole, and joyful you. That is God's powerful but tender invitation as He deeply desires to help us move us from pain to perspective. Will you trust Him to put together all the parts of your life?

Key Learnings:

- Pain is the number one reason we move to living out of our heads instead of our hearts.
- Like splinters, pain will not be a one-time experience in our lives. We will need to deal with it on an ongoing basis.
- You can only shut off so many parts of your heart until all that's left is a shell.
- As God is, so life is. How we see God is the filter through which we see life.
- When we are not intentional about choosing change, by default, we are choosing chaos.
- Given that most things in our life may not change, the only thing that can is our perspective.
- If I have to be in control of everything then all I can ever have is what I can manufacture. That leaves no room for what God can do.

Questions to Consider:

1. What have you given up by choosing to live out of your head instead of your heart?

2. Can you remember a time in your life when you felt the doors in your heart slamming shut?

3. How have you compartmentalized your life?

4. What holds you back from agreeing with God that He has the right to orchestrate the events of your life?

5. Do you truly believe God is good?

6. How do you let your spirit catch up with your body?

7. How have you chosen to cope with your chaos?

8. How would you describe the wake of your life?

Passages to Ponder:

"I will give you a new heart and put a new spirit in you; I will remove from you your heart of stone and give you a heart of flesh" (Ezekiel 36:26 NIV).

"I know the Lord is always with me, I will not be shaken, for He is right beside me" (Psalm 16:8).

"I am overcome with joy because of God's unfailing love, for He has seen my troubles and He cares about the anguish of my soul" (Psalm 31:7).

"God is our refuge and strength, always ready to help in times of trouble" (Psalm 46:1).

"Though I am surrounded by troubles, You will protect me from the anger of my enemies. You reach out Your hand, and the power of Your right hand saves me. The LORD will work out His plans for my life—for Your faithful love, O LORD, endures forever" (Psalm 138:7-8).

Prayer of Invitation:

Gracious God,

I invite you into my pain. Forgive me for trying to manage it on my own. Please change my heart. Help me to receive all the love You want to pour into it. Help me to trust You and Your Word. Cause hope to arise within me. Show me the next steps I need to take to move from my pain to Your perspective. Grant me uncommon power, strength, and grace I pray. Amen.

Practice Point:

Because pain will not be a one-time experience in our lives, we will need to deal with it on an ongoing basis. The next time you mow the lawn, load the dishwasher, or wash your car, let it serve as a reminder to check to see if there's any junk in your heart that needs to be cleaned out to alleviate the pain it is causing.

If you have trusted friends in your life, consider asking them what it is like to lie in the wake of your life? ie. What ripples do you initiate that they feel? (positive and negative)

Chapter 5

The Satisfied Heart: Moving from Entitled To Expectant

B y now you may be feeling a great deal of mixed emotions at the concepts and principles we have been discussing. If you're not, be grateful. If you are, be grateful! God is working in you, stirring your heart and drawing you into a deeper relationship with Himself. Going deeper with God means inviting more of Him into our lives which inevitably leaves less room for our own sin and selfishness. In this chapter, we want to look at another internal shift that is vital to living with our hearts at rest—moving from entitled to expectant.

To be **entitled** is an expression of forcing God's hand, suggesting that God is required to hear our prayers and meet our expectations, in the way He answers them. An entitled heart says, "After all I've been through, I deserve a little something good to come my way" or "Why can't I have _____ I've earned it" Those who consider themselves to be *have nots* may think that life (and God for that matter) has been unfair. This way of thinking often leads to justifying a victim mentality. Others express a sense of privilege by suggesting that because they have prayed a certain way for a specific request, God is somehow obligated to respond in absolute alignment with their appeal for His help. God is viewed more like a vending machine than Almighty God, the Sovereign Creator of the universe. Scripture clearly invites us to ask of God and to stand on the promises of His Word, but it provides counsel on the prerequisite to our petitions. "But when you ask him, *be sure that your faith is in God alone.* Do not waver, for a person with divided loyalty is as unsettled as a wave of the sea that is blown and tossed by the wind. Such people should not expect to receive anything from the Lord. Their loyalty is divided between God and the world, and they are unstable in everything they do" (James 1:6-8). [Emphasis Mine] Scripture is very direct on this matter. James, who was writing to a predominantly Jewish audience, wanted to make certain that his readers understood that their faith was to be entirely in God—not their heritage, their manner of praying, their diligent religious activity, or even in their personal faith. The only acceptable object of their faith was reserved for God alone. Paul echoes that thought in 1 Corinthians 2:5 where he states, "Your faith should not be in the wisdom of men but in the power of God."

A sense of entitlement is certainly not foreign to those mature in their faith. In fact, many who have walked with the Lord for a number of years and have served Him faithfully can experience an unspoken and unresolved sense of disillusionment as, over time, they become "weary in well doing." While they may not articulate it this way, they expect they should be past some of the trials they're still going through, that they've experienced enough pain for one lifetime, or that God should be rewarding them in some way for their faithfulness. Their private ruminations might go something like this,

"God, I think I've had more than my share. You have allowed more heartache in my life than most other people I know. You can change my circumstances if You want to – why don't You? What else do you want from me? I've walked faithfully with you for years, when does it get easier?" Ongoing family and financial struggles are classic examples of unrelenting issues that wear us down mentally, physically, emotionally, and spiritually. In those extended seasons, it is easy

to become disenchanted in our walk with God, and if we don't guard our hearts, we can effortlessly spiral back into woundedness. Left unattended, this unsettled anger plants seeds of exasperation in our hearts that, often unknowingly, grow into a silent but all-encompassing sense of resentment. Such bitterness casts a shadow over every part of our lives. Irrespective of what we've been through or how long we've walked with God, a grudge against Him for allowing difficult and painful things to happen in our lives is often at the root of our sense of entitlement.

Conversely, to be **expectant is** an expression of faith, anchored in our trust in God's goodness and His power. Expectancy reflects an understanding that God has heard our prayers and believes He will answer, but He gets to decide when and how. We eagerly embrace His response, knowing it truly is best, even when we don't understand. "In the morning, Lord, You hear my voice; in the morning I lay my requests before You and wait expectantly" (Psalm 5:3). " I eagerly expect and hope that I will in no way be ashamed, but will have sufficient courage so that now as always Christ will be exalted in my body, whether by life or by death" (Philippians 1:20).

We find joy in our hearts and rest in our souls when we live with an attitude of expectancy about God's character and His desire for our lives—both of which enable us, not entitle us.

Let's consider the consequences of expectations we may not even realize we have. Unrealistic expectations are the rocks the enemy ties around our necks as we try to swim through life. They drown our souls and leave us frantically flailing for physical, emotional, and spiritual air. Our loved ones are often the ones who feel the impact of the waves created by our flailing. Unfortunately, I know only too well the price to be paid for perpetually high standards and the havoc it wreaks on our hearts, our health, and our homes. The greater the distance between our expectations and our reality, the greater the angst in our souls. I am very familiar with angst in my soul. I liken it to the analogy of someone standing on your emotional and spiritual air hose. I cannot tell you how many times my soul has silently screamed, *get off my air hose; I can't breathe.* Over time I am learning to invite God into those moments, asking

Him to show me the view beyond what I can see from my limited vantage point.

I believe when we recognize and learn to identify the unworkable standards we set for God, ourselves, and others, we are well on our way to untying the asphyxiating rocks in our lives that block the free-flowing wind of God's Spirit. "For the Lord is the Spirit and wherever the Spirit of the Lord is, there is freedom" (2 Corinthians 3:17).

Unspoken Expectations

If we took a closer look at our lives, we would find a host of unspoken expectations that feed the insatiable appetite of entitlement. Consider what your expectations are in the following areas:

Expectations of God. I think it is safe to say that we have expectations of God to be kind, good, gracious, and loving. His Word tells us in Psalm 145:9, "The Lord is good to everyone. He showers compassion on all his creation," and many of us have experienced that to be true. The angst in our soul begins to swell when our sense of entitlement begins to dictate the way we feel God should demonstrate His kindness, goodness, grace, and love to us. Our hearts are happy to receive the encouragement the above scriptures provide. However, our hearts tend to bristle a little when we read passages such as, "All Scripture is inspired by God and is useful to teach us what is true and to make us realize what is wrong in our lives. It corrects us when we are wrong and teaches us to do what is right" (2 Timothy 3:16). "For the LORD corrects those he loves, just as a father corrects a child in whom he delights" (Proverbs 3:12 NIV). "Blessed is the one whom God corrects; so do not despise the discipline of the Almighty" (Job 5:17 NIV).

As parents, it's easy to see the correlation between love and discipline. Yet, we somehow feel we have outgrown the need for that in our own lives. There is no verse in the Bible to suggest we ever outgrow our need for God's discipline. In fact, the greatest gift we give our children, even when they are adults, is to model our own vibrant, growing relationship with Christ. That includes yielding to His ongoing discipline in our own lives. The principles of pruning and correction described in John 15 do not expire until God calls us Home. Until then, He invites us to embrace a paradigm shift in our thinking. A shift that recalibrates the posture of our heart so it can receive what it needs most – God's grace. Humility is a mark of spiritual maturity but is, sadly, the road less traveled in many of our homes and churches. 1 Peter 5:5 reminds us that "God opposes the proud, but gives grace to the humble."

Expectations of yourself. "I just need to be more organized, figure this out, lose some weight, be more disciplined. I should be better at…" We can often replay messages like these and others in our heads when life is not playing out how we expected it to. We see where we don't measure up (at least in our minds) and so we set the bar higher for ourselves as we chase the elusive goal of 'getting it right' or being good enough. Instead of bringing the release we're looking for, it just adds bricks to the baggage we carry through life. Comparison sends it into overdrive. Comparing ourselves with others is a common, and unfortunately effective, tool used by the enemy that holds us hostage - bound up in insecurity and demanding an unquenchable ransom of 'do more, get more, be more.'

Be careful not to worship at the altar of "getting it right" or "getting it all together" lest you leave the altar empty or you miss "it" altogether. Living with no regrets can only happen when you live by the principles of God's Word and follow the plan He has laid out for your life. He is the only One Who can help us make peace with our humanness.

When we have expectations of ourselves that we can clean up our act, getting the dirt out of our own souls, it is evidence of a sense of entitlement that is rooted in pride. Pride that we can do this on our own and we don't need God. David, who understood well what it was like to try and make life work on his own, reminds us in Psalm 19: 12–14 "How can I know all the sins lurking in my heart? Cleanse me from these hidden faults. Keep me from deliberate sins! Don't let them control me. Then I will be free of guilt and innocent of great sin. May the words of my mouth and the thoughts of my heart be pleasing to you, O Lord, my rock and my redeemer."

Expectations of your spouse. God expects certain behaviors from husbands and wives as foundations for a healthy marriage—namely faithfulness, fidelity, selfless love, and genuine respect. (Ephesians 5:22-25, 33). And it is true that God designed us to live in community where we can meet others' needs and they reach out to meet ours. That's why God created different personalities. He knew we would need each other's strengths (and weaknesses) so that we could mutually encourage one another and build into each other's lives. While that was God's plan, we don't always live it out as He desires. We read in James 3:2, "we all stumble in many ways." It seems that we find it much easier to extend grace to those who live in our community than it is to those who live inside our home. Instead of setting kindness as the standard, we set unattainable expectations in an attempt to satisfy all of our heart's desires. But, our spouses were never intended to meet all of our needs. Some of them yes but not all of them.

We must be careful not to make the pedestal too high for our spouses because if we do, there's not much room for them to move before they fall off. When they do, they often crash into a field of land mines where everything blows up and nothing they do is good enough. Best-selling marriage and family author, Gary Thomas, regularly poses a radically re-orienting question in his *Sacred Marriage* seminars. He asks, "What if God's design for marriage was not to teach us how to feel loved but to teach us how to love?" I firmly believe that our spouses are God's primary human tool for sharpening our character.

Expectations of your kids. To be sure, the suggestion that a sense of entitlement is epidemic amongst the youth in our world today is not a novel idea. The question in my mind that begs to be asked is "How did I/do I contribute to that sense of entitlement?" It is in our desire to make things better for our children than we had for ourselves. Our desire to create more opportunities or help remove some of the struggle, has in fact, had the opposite of its intended effect. We assumed that our *gift* to them would be received with our understanding of what it took to provide that gift. However, it's not realistic to expect children to understand the effort it takes if they've never had to work for, or sacrifice anything. Something intangible but very necessary happens in the process of struggle that is lost when the struggle is removed. It's like helping a butterfly as it wrenches its way out of its cocoon. By removing the cocoon, we may feel we've helped the butterfly attain freedom, but the truth is, we've robbed is of its ability to fly. Its wings only become usable by the workout they get through the wrenching process.

The role we as parents play in the development of our children's attitudes about God, greed, and gratitude cannot be overstated. As the adage goes, "more is caught than is taught." Children are bombarded by the influences of the world, their flesh, and the devil. We serve our children best when we model attitudes that become the basis for God-honoring actions.

Expectations of your church. God's desire is that our churches be places for people to be taught the truth of His Word, nurtured in our faith, and encouraged in our walk with Christ. Churches are to be places where we are filled up but also where we pour into others. Otherwise, we can feel entitled to entertainment. If we only come on Sunday mornings to *get our fix*, we miss out on all that God has for us as He works through us to touch the hearts and lives of others in significant ways. We also become extremely susceptible to spiritual consumerism, which opens the door for the enemy to tempt us to treat church like a spiritual smörgåsbord where we only participate in the activities we like and leave untouched endeavors we don't like. Becoming a spectator gives birth to a critical spirit which becomes toxic to our souls, our homes, our relationships, and the church where we come to enjoy God and His family.

Expectations of others – other people or other activities. "My soul finds rest in God alone" (Psalm 62:1 NIV). God is jealous for our attention and affection. "You must not bow down to them or worship them, for I, the LORD your God, am a jealous God who will not tolerate your affection for any other gods" (Exodus 20:5). He wants us to come to Him for what we need and not look to any other source. Any other source is a false god. We might vehemently deny our belief in false gods, but when you boil it all down, going to other people, places, or pursuits to get what God alone can give us reveals one of two things: either we don't believe He can or will provide what we need, or we aren't prepared to surrender to His plan for receiving it. Either way, we are putting our faith in something/someone other than God. That makes it a false god. "You must worship no other gods, for the LORD, whose very name is Jealous, is a God who is jealous about his relationship with you" (Exodus 34:14). God wants all of your heart, not just part of it. That's why He pursues it so intensely.

Scripture gives us a sense of expectancy and takes away our sense of entitled expectation. When we hear the cries of the people in Scripture coupled with their expressions of praise, it builds our faith.

We Should Expect:

Change. Just as there are changes in the seasons, there are changes in the seasons of our life and the seasons of our soul. During these seasons, our capacity will fluctuate. When I look back on the days of working and raising kids, with the additional demands of my children's special needs and my husband working out of town, I sometimes wonder how I managed to shoot up a quick prayer, never mind read my Bible and spend time in God's presence. I used to think those days/years would never end, but they did. They always end. Looking back, the days were long, but the years were short. Now as I spend quiet nights at home, I wonder where the time went. Just as winter is often a dark season where you don't see much growth (at least not where I live), the splendor of spring reveals what has happened undetected underground. Fresh sights, sounds, smells, and colors re-invigorate our spirits and renew our sense of hope in the newness and freshness of life. Routine is the soil in which habits grow—good or bad. If we plant quality seeds and uphold worthy habits in the winter seasons, spring will be all the more magnificent!

To get it wrong sometimes. I'm not suggesting we have an out for our poor choices. I'm acknowledging that we will make poor choices. "The Spirit is willing but the flesh is weak" (Mark 14:38). God never intended that we should get everything right this side of eternity. If we could, we wouldn't be human, we wouldn't need God, and why would we want or need to go to heaven? Romans 3:10 tells us, "there is none righteous, no not one." That includes you. That includes me. Despite our heart for God and our very best efforts and intentions, we will still get it wrong sometimes. The senior pastor at our church often says, "It's not the perfection of your life; it's the direction of it that matters." Holding ourselves hostage to unrealistic expectations just keeps the internal turmoil revving and zaps the joy from our lives. The mental and emotional gymnastics we put ourselves through are not God's heart or desire for us. "He has not given us a spirit of fear, but of power, love and a sound mind" (2 Timothy 1:7). Once again, there is a better way to live. "Peace I leave with you; My peace I give to you. Not as the world gives, give I to you" (John 14:27).

The enemy's attack. John 8:44 tells us Satan is "the father of all lies." When pain happens in our lives, Satan loves to tell us we did something to deserve the pain. That lie needs to be exposed from the beginning. Remember our conversation about beating ourselves up over wrong choices/decisions suggests that God's ability to work in our circumstances is limited to our choices? Scripture tells us in Psalm 103:6, 8-12 that, "The LORD is compassionate and merciful, slow to get angry and filled with unfailing love. He will not constantly accuse us, nor remain angry forever. **He does not punish us for all our sins; He does not deal harshly with us, as we deserve.** For His unfailing love toward those who fear Him is as great as the height of the heavens above the earth. He has removed our sins as far from us as the east is from the west." [Emphasis Mine] It is true that some of the hardships in our lives are of our own doing, but as we can see from the above passage, even then, God is gracious.

Our flesh warring against us. Certainly, the enemy comes to steal our joy, kill our hope, and destroy our peace (John 10:10), but we can't blame him when we need to take responsibility. Paul, a man who whole-heartedly and passionately followed Christ and through whom God chose to write more than half of the New Testament, knew only too well the struggle against his own sinful nature. In Romans 7: 18–21, we get a glimpse into the humanity which plagued his heart and continues to beleaguer ours. "For I know that good itself does not dwell in me, that is, in my sinful nature. For I have the desire to do what is good, but I cannot carry it out. For I do not do the good I want to do, but the evil I do not want to do—this I keep on doing. Now if I do what I do not want to do, it is no longer I who do it, but it is sin living in me that does it. So I find this law at work: Although I want to do good, evil is right there with me" (NIV). I'm so glad this passage is in the Bible. It helps me better understand my inner wrestlings. It also makes me so grateful for the cross because that's where the power of sin was dealt its mortal blow. "For sin is the sting that results in death, and the law gives sin its power. But thank God! He gives us victory over sin and death through our Lord Jesus Christ" (I Corinthians 15:56,57).

Replacing Entitlement with Grace

Often during or shortly after a season of intense grief or suffering, there is a desire to extend grace to people because of their circumstances. While that is absolutely appropriate, we need to be careful not to contribute to an attitude of entitlement in the process. I saw this often with our son Randy. Because of his Cerebral Palsy, people would excuse his poor behavior, lower their expectations of what he could/should do, and help him do things he was capable of doing on his own. Although they thought they were helping him, they were crippling him further. God calls us to extend grace but we must ask His wisdom so we are not unintentionally enabling those we desire to comfort.

Sometimes grace looks like untying ourselves and others from those unrealistic expectations. Other times it looks like simple patience—with ourselves and with others. And sometimes, it looks like granting people favor when they don't deserve it. Just like God grants favor to us.

Gratitude's Unexpected Power

It's easy to think of the words *thank you* simply as good manners. However, the following story by Joni Eareckson Tada, who has been confined to a wheelchair for more than five decades as the result of a diving accident, shows us otherwise.

"Giving thanks to God for my life and the events of my days may come supernaturally to me now, but it wasn't always this way.

After I was released from the hospital, my sister invited me to come live with her on our Maryland farm. Still a teenager and new to my wheelchair, I wondered what my new life as a quadriplegic would be. Often, my sister parked me in my chair next to the big bay window that overlooked the pasture. Everything in me wanted to be on my feet, outside, walking into the barn, feeding the horse, and saddling up for a ride. And yes, at that moment, I was feeling very sorry for myself.

But even in those days I knew that daydreaming and fantasizing about such things would only make my attitude worse. I'd had enough of dark depression when I was in the hospital and didn't want to go down that grim path to despair again. So, sitting there by the window, looking out at the morning sunlight on that Maryland pasture, I remember praying a prayer that went something like this:

'Jesus, my mind-set today is like a stubborn horse that doesn't want to be saddled up and led out of the barn. My attitude is stiff-necked and obstinate, but I am not going to let it win this day. My spirit within me wants to do what's right, so I'm putting spurs on my attitude today. I'm going to goad it out of the barn into the light of day and down a path of gratitude. My feelings don't want to go there; I'd rather stay in my dark stall. But with Your help, I'm going to whip my feelings in the right direction. And as I do....please, Lord, give me a grateful attitude. Help me not only to do but also to feel the right thing.' I wanted God to shed His light on a new path. And He did. Over time, God changed those feelings and gave me an attitude of genuine, heartfelt gratitude. Nothing or no one else could have changed me from the inside out like that. It had to be me in partnership with God's powerful Holy Spirit."[14]

I had the privilege of spending some time with Joni at a Special Needs conference that our church hosted. She made a comment that has stuck with me and created a paradigm shift in my thinking. In one of our discussions, she matter-of-factly stated that she *had to thank Jesus every day for her life and circumstances.* I remember thinking at the time, you don't *have* to offer gratitude to God throughout your day; that's a choice you make. Certainly, thanksgiving is one option among many, but in the months that followed our conversation, I came to understand why intentional gratitude really is the only option that matters. We aren't grateful for the things we think we deserve. Without deliberately focusing on all that God is, has, and does in light of what we aren't, don't have, and can't do, we are exposed and vulnerable to the attacks of the world, the flesh, and the devil. We've all been dragged down those dark roads by the harsh taskmaster of ingratitude. Once again, I remind you, there is a better way to live. The simple but unnatural discipline of daily saying "thank you" to God for His goodness, grace, faithfulness, power, provision, protection, and His unshakable presence, works in us the inside out transformation we desire. It's like a treasure hunt, forcing us to look for evidence of God's character in our days. It's also a practical way to fix our eyes on Jesus. But as Joni notes, it only happens *over time* as we walk and work in tandem with God's powerful Holy Spirit. As we purposefully focus our thoughts on God's character and His goodness while "putting the spurs" to our sense of entitlement, God will forge an attitude of gratitude within our souls. That creates a culture of expectancy in which feelings of unencumbered joy and deep seated peace can bud, blossom, and grow.

Key Learnings:

❤ Unrealistic expectations are the rocks the enemy ties around our necks as we try to swim through life. They drown our souls and leave us frantically flailing for physical, emotional, and spiritual air. Our loved ones are often the ones who feel the impact of the waves created by our flailing.

❤ Something intangible, but very necessary, happens in the process of struggle that is lost when the struggle is removed.

❤ Scripture gives us a sense of expectancy and takes away our sense of entitled expectation.

❤ Routine is the soil in which habits grow—good or bad.

❤ We aren't grateful for what we think we deserve.

Questions to Consider:

1. What expectations do you have of God? Are you holding a grudge against Him for not meeting them?

2. Are there unrealistic expectations in your life/relationships? Do you need to untie yourself from these?

3. What is your response to the idea that God's design for marriage is not to teach us how to feel loved but to teach us how to love?

4. Are there ways in which your desire to extend grace has become enabling versus empowering?

5. How do you need to "put the spurs" to your sense of entitlement?

Passages to Ponder:

"But when you ask Him, be sure that you really expect Him to answer, for a doubtful mind is as unsettled as a wave of the sea that is tossed by the wind. People like that should not expect to receive anything from the Lord. They can't make up their minds. They waver back and forth in everything they do" (James 1:6-8).

"God sets Himself against the proud, but He shows favor to the humble. So humble yourselves before God. Resist the Devil, and he will flee from you. Draw close to God, and God will draw close to you. Wash your hands, you sinners; purify your hearts, you hypocrites" (James 4:6-8).

"Listen to my voice in the morning, Lord. Each morning I bring my requests to you and wait expectantly" (Psalm 5:3).

Prayer of Invitation:

Lord Jesus,

Thank You for loving me even when I have heart attitudes that don't honor You. I confess my sense of entitlement and ask You to forgive me for trying to make You do things my way. Show me where I have unrealistic expectations of You, myself, and others. Help me set realistic goals in their place. Plant seeds of gratitude in my heart I pray. Help me to water them with Your Word and intentional expressions of thankfulness for Your goodness and Your power in my life.

May it all be by Your grace and for Your glory, Amen.

Practice Point:

Select one or two verses from the "Passages to Ponder" section in this chapter and commit to memorizing them over the next week. Write them out, put a notification on your phone to review them each day, and speak them out loud so you can hear the truth and let it soak into your soul.

Practice fixing your eyes on Jesus this week by choosing a characteristic of God, eg. kindness, and then thank Him for all the ways you can see His kindness in the day. Write some of your thoughts in a journal. They will encourage you later.

Chapter Six

The Strengthened Heart: Letting Praise Anchor Your Soul

I like to read. My overflowing bookcases and the stacks of reading material beside my bed can attest to that. Given the plethora of great books to read and the fullness of my life, other than Scripture, precious few are the books I go back to read again. There is one, however, that I have read eight to ten times each year for the past number of years. It is a book by Stormie Omartian entitled, *The Prayer That Changes Everything: The Hidden Power of Praising God*. I admit the title made me a little skeptical when I first saw it but I have since mined countless gems of truth from its pages that have dramatically altered the way I interact with my Heavenly Father and radically re-framed my pattern of response to the events of my life. The book has 30 chapters, one for each day of the month; it is chocked full of scripture, and it includes a personal prayer pertaining to each chapter's content. As I meet with people, particularly those who are reeling in response to overwhelming circumstances or those struggling with stronghold issues, I recommend they get a copy and begin to let God use it to bring freedom and wholeness to their lives. The book's impact on my life cannot be overstated.

Work Over Worship

Growing up on the farm, with parents who had a strong work ethic meant that considerable emphasis was put on teaching my brother and me how to work but considerably less emphasis was put on teaching us how to worship. However, I don't believe my parent's mindset was, or is, unique to those raised in rural settings or even to those in committed relationships with Christ. Much of the teaching in many of our churches is focused on teaching us about and equipping us for kingdom work. This teaching is a good thing. But it may be at the expense of educating us in the core significance of kingdom worship. A disproportionate emphasis on how to be pouring our lives out in service of God and others without training and modeling the need for the replenishment of our souls has left many God fearing, faithful followers depleted, discouraged, and wanting. This vulnerability of soul makes them prime targets for the enemy's lies and schemes. Ironically, worship—the act of coming into God's presence to give Him praise—has long since been considered an *extra* or a *filler* in our worship services. However, worship is God's primary design for replenishing our souls.

My parents certainly never stood in the way of my desire to be involved in church activities but other than singing songs at church and paying my tithe as an act of worship, I had little understanding of its importance or power. I didn't know it could become a way of doing life that would radically shift the posture of my heart and impact my entire perspective, especially during the dark seasons of my soul. I had read that "God inhabits the praises of His people" (Psalm 22:3), but I had no idea of the influence praise could have on my everyday life.

In addition, I couldn't seem to crack the mystery around *coming into God's presence*. I felt like I was on the outside looking in "through a glass darkly" (1 Corinthians 13:12 KJV) trying to ascertain what coming into God's presence actually meant. I wasn't sure what I was hoping to find, I just knew I hadn't found it yet. Sometimes it's easy to watch others and surmise that coming into God's presence looks one particular way or another. I've since learned it was my lack of understanding that complicated the notion, for there is no secret code or special performance required. It is simply extending an invitation to God to join you as you do life—moment by moment. My head understood the concept, but in my heart, there was something lacking. The missing piece for me was coming to the realization that, while my head desired to be in God's presence, the access point for my heart was through praise. Words of praise, spoken or sung, allow my head and heart to move in tandem towards God. It was not until reading *The Prayer That Changes Everything* that I began to understand the profound strengthening of our hearts and anchoring of our souls that takes place when we personalize our expressions of praise to God and allow praise to be our first response, no matter what. Stormie Omartian explains it like this:

> "Worship and praise is the purest form of prayer because it focuses our minds and souls entirely away from ourselves and on to Him…When we worship God, we are the closest to Him we will ever be. That's because praise welcomes His presence in our midst…When we worship and praise God, His presence comes to dwell with us. And the most amazing thing about that is when it does, things change. Always! You can count on it. Hearts change. Situations change. Lives change. Minds change. Attitudes change. Every time you praise God, something changes within you, or your circumstances, or in the people or situations around you …. The reason for that is you are coming in contact with all that God is and that will affect all that you are."[15]

She goes on to say,
> "Every time we praise God for who He is and all that He has done, it unleashes His life-changing power in our lives. His presence comes to soften our hearts so they can be molded into whatever shape HE wants. Praise is the

means by which God transforms our lives and enables us to do His will and glorify Him."[16]

I have seen this precept borne out in my life many times. It was especially valuable during a turbulent season in my marriage. The more I leaned into and praised God for Who He was and what He could do, the more the scales came off my heart and God's resurrection power breathed reconciliation and vibrancy into our relationship.

I want to be clear that praising God is not some magic formula to get God to do what you want. "Praise becomes the very means by which God pours Himself into our lives. It's not something we can manipulate God into doing. It's a gift to those who have a true heart of love and reverence for Him. Only those who put God first will uncover the hidden power of praise."[17] Stormie offers a poignant reminder.

> "God's power is not cheap. Just like the electric power that comes into our homes, there is a price to pay for it. Only the price is not monetary. The price is spending time to fill ourselves with God's Word so we can *understand* the power. It's praying so we can *access* the power. It's living in obedience so we can *maximize* the power. It's praising and worshiping God so that we *open up the lines* through which God's power flows into our lives."[18]

It is "opening up of the lines" that brings it altogether. When we read our Bibles, spend time in prayer, and live a life of obedience and still feel disconnected from God, it is easy to become disillusioned and even bitter. Furthermore, it makes us increasingly susceptible to the lies of the enemy that God is not good nor does He care. Praising God helps us to "guard our hearts" (Proverbs 4:23) and life in the truth of Who His Word says He is and what He can do in our lives.

Plastic Worship

As I have mentioned earlier, I am a very pragmatic person and am often skeptical of people who try to manufacture an emotional experience in a worship context. Even now, while I've become much more free and forthcoming in my praise, I would not consider myself to be an expressive worshiper. That's just not who I am. That being said, I've wrestled many times with feeling like I'm being fake when my desire truly is to worship God, but I don't sense His presence and I'm only giving lip service to words I'm singing or saying. Perhaps you can relate. I remind myself as I remind you, our feelings don't dictate God's truth and it is in times like these that our head needs to lead our heart. We need to make the conscious decision that our faith is not based on our feelings. "If you don't sense His presence in your life, praise and worship Him until you do. That's not trying to manipulate God, it's breaking down your own barriers in order to allow Him access to your waiting heart."[19] I've discovered there are many barriers which can clog the lines to my heart—distraction, worry, a desire to fix things on my own, unconfessed sin, and not pouring out my pain to God, just to name a few. Persisting in praise acts like a spiritual *Drano*, shifting the posture of my heart and opening up the lines that allow God to pour His peace, power and presence into me.

Shifting the Posture of Your Heart

Shifting the posture of your heart is like a railway switch that once tripped opens the way for the train to take a different path—one that often avoids a train wreck. Both tracks are headed in the same general direction, but they lead to distinct destinations with equally different outcomes. When we allow praise to become a lifestyle that re-frames our patterns of response to the happenings of our lives, it becomes the switch that opens up the way for us to choose a better way to live. What could that look like? It might look like praising God as your Provider when finances are tight; it might look like praising Him as your Redeemer when you or someone you love has made poor choices that seem irreparable.

It might be thanking Him that He is your Deliverer when you seem stalled in overwhelming circumstances that you fear may take you under. Praise helps us thank Him that He has a plan for our lives, even (and especially) when we can't see it. A lifestyle of praise may simply be praising Him for His love and forgiveness that you have received. Praise moves your heart from entitled to expectant, from frustrated to faith filled, from grouchy to grateful. Praise does all this and so much more. However, I cannot stress enough that this is not an exercise in the power of positive thinking, but rather heartfelt statements of surrender to the sovereignty of God. They are words of affirmation of God's character and power and they reflect an understanding of His intense desire to be with us in both the raucous and routine moments of our lives. "You can't overcome negative thoughts with good thoughts. The battle between the two will rage on forever. You have to combat bad thoughts with the Word of God, prayer and praise."[20]

The clearest way I know how to explain what happens when we make worship our first response in times of crisis, is that it moves our prayers from frantic cries of desperation to a place where we can humbly, but confidently invite God to come and do what only He can in our current situation. It's the difference between "help me God, please, please help me" to "Thank You Lord that You know what I need and that You are more than able to provide it." Both are asking God for His help but one comes from a place of depletion, the other from an anchored heart. Simply put, the shortest route from panic to peace is through praise. It is what creates that subtle, but oh so crucial, shift in the posture of your heart that allows you to fall back to sleep at night knowing that God is willing and more than able to supply whatever is needed to address the concerns replaying in your mind.

I am not suggesting there is a quick and easy gratitude mantra that will immediately and permanently dissolve all fear and pain from your life. Nor am I implying that this is a quick-fix way to live in denial of your circumstances. Instead, choosing to let worship and praise become your new pattern of response reveals an intentional choice to "look at the reality of your life *straight on* and declare an *even greater reality* straight over it"[21] A response that invites all of Who God is and what He can do to come to bear on your situation. It demonstrates your heart's resolve to "put on the garment of praise for the spirit of heaviness" (Isaiah 61:3) knowing that "God's purposes will prevail" (Proverbs 19:21 NIV) and that you choose His wisdom and ways over your own.

I believe that at their core, our anxious moments are really our heart's invitation to worship—to be reminded of God's goodness, power, and intimate interest and care for our lives. Otherwise, "prayer can sometimes become an excuse for allowing anxiety to churn in our hearts. Rather than directing our thoughts to God, we direct them to whatever is troubling us. It's no surprise, then, that we come away still feeling fearful. That's what happened when Pastor Charles Stanley began to pray with a woman whose husband was undergoing surgery. As the woman prayed, Stanley realized that her prayers were becoming more frantic by the second. "Her total focus," he noted, "was on her husband and the operation—none of her focus was truly on God as the Great Physician .... I interrupted her prayer and said, 'Ma'am. We need to focus on what God can do in that operating room. We need to focus on Who He is and what He is capable of doing.'" "I praised God," he says, "for His great love of her husband and of her, of His absolute authority over everything in that hospital, of His wisdom that could manifest itself in every move the surgeon made ... and when I said amen, I saw in her eyes the peace of God, rather than the sheer panic that had been there just minutes before."[22]

Worship While You Wait

We've all felt like the psalmist, "How long, O Lord, will You forget me? Forever? How long will you look the other way? How long must I struggle with anguish in my soul, with sorrow in my heart every day? How long will my enemy have the upper hand? Turn and answer me, O Lord, my God! Restore the light to my eyes or I will die" (Psalm 13:1-3). At times like these, we need to train our hearts to lean into worship. It will not come instinctively.

In our flesh, our hearts are not naturally bent towards God. We are born with a sinful nature. Worship helps remind us of who God is and what He is capable of; He has not forgotten, we are the ones that need the reminder. Worship helps us remember. "Let all that I am praise the LORD; may I never forget the good things He does for me" (Psalm 103:2).

A dear friend of mine coined the phrase, "worship while you wait" as a way to coach our hearts when God's answers to our prayers seem delayed or postponed. Those words have often got my heart and soul back on track when they've been derailed by fear, anger, frustration, impatience, or lack of direction.

Worship as A Weapon

Joshua chapter six records the story of the fall of the walls of Jericho. Albeit a fun Sunday School story to act out, it has much to teach us about the power of worship. Picking up the story in verse 8 we read, "After Joshua spoke to the people, the seven priests with the rams' horns started marching in the presence of the LORD, blowing the horns as they marched. And the Ark of the LORD's Covenant followed behind them. Some of the armed men marched in front of the priests with the horns and some behind the Ark, with the priests continually blowing the horns. 'Do not shout; do not even talk,' Joshua commanded. 'Not a single word from any of you until I tell you to shout. Then shout!'... On the seventh day the Israelites got up at dawn and marched around the city as they had done before. But this time they went around the city seven times. The seventh time around as the priests sounded the long blasts on their horns, Joshua commanded the people, 'Shout! For the Lord has given you the city!' When the people heard the sounds of the horns, they shouted as loud as they could. Suddenly, the walls of Jericho collapsed and the Israelites charged straight into the city from every side and captured it" (Joshua 6:8-10, 15, 16, 20).

Of the wealth of principles that this passage provides, I would like to highlight a couple. First, God's plan all along for defeating this formidable foe of the Israelites was simply worship, not military might, not an undercover ambush, nor a clever deception.

Nope, just out-in-the-open, before-your-eyes worship. Ponder for a moment what God is demonstrating in this passage about the power of worship and its ability to bring down the strongholds in your life.

Horns were one of the primary worship instruments used in Hebrew culture, but given that they were the only weapon the priests had, I have to admit, I would have felt pretty defenseless and vulnerable had I been asked to fall in line behind that priestly parade. Imagining myself in the story, makes me think of Psalm 20:7, "Some trust in chariots and some in horses, but we will remember the name of the Lord our God" (KJV). In the absence of horses and chariots, those who marched would have no doubt been focused on the need for the power in the name of the Lord, their God. Scripture records that as they worshiped and obeyed, God brought not only deliverance, but victory. May I remind you once again, that God *inhabits* the praises of His people. That's where He lives and in that place, there is no room for the enemy or his influence! Worship is indeed a powerful spiritual weapon.

Second, notice that they were told not to talk, "not a single word from any of you until I tell you to shout." At first glance, Joshua can be perceived as a bit of a control freak or a bit naïve to think, "if we're quiet, they may not know we're here," but I don't believe either of those notions to be true. He passed to the people the marching orders, (literally) that he received from the Lord. I believe they were asked to be silent to create room for God to speak to the fear and reservations in their hearts. Once again, as I imagine myself in the story, I understand myself well enough to know I'd be thinking something along the lines of, "I wonder if Joshua has thought about ..." or "God's never done it like this before, I wonder what Joshua's Plan B looks like." By day five or six, I can hear myself saying, "My feet hurt," or "This is ridiculous, all this marching has accomplished nothing." As my frustration level rose, so might my anxiety, "What if the wall doesn't come down like Joshua said it would?" "God, why did You bring me here in the first place?" "God, can I really trust You?" I am certain those, and a myriad of other thoughts, flooded the minds of the Israelites on the six days of their muted march. I'm also sure that while they really wanted to trust in the power of Almighty God, sometimes it was hard. Only during those times of silence was God able to speak His peace, power, and presence into their conflicted hearts.

There are times when God wants us to be silent before Him and doing so is an act of worship. Rather than trying to manage life and manufacture solutions in our strength, we need to make a conscious act of surrender to be silent before Him. Have you ever talked with someone who was asking for advice but wouldn't stop talking long enough to hear what advice you had to give them? That's often the way we are when we come before God. It's not that we have to be still *all* the time, but *some* of the time for sure. "We need times when we simply come before Him quietly in worship. To be still before Him. To simply rest in His presence."[23] Being quiet long enough to let Him address the longings in our hearts is doing an uncommon thing in order to achieve an uncommon result. When we do, we increase our capacity to grasp the extent of His capacity to meet us in our need. We make room for Him to speak into our hearts what we are desperately waiting to hear. Words like, "I see you my child," or "You are not forgotten," or "I have a plan and it will be glorious," or "Trust Me, I know what you need."

Worship, especially worship that draws on the truth and power of God's Word, is one of our greatest weapon against all of the enemies of our soul—the world, the flesh, and the devil. John 4:23 reminds us, "But the time is coming—indeed it's here now—when true worshipers will worship the Father in spirit and in truth." The Father is looking for those who will worship Him that way.

If you're still wondering, where do I begin? check out *Passages to Ponder* at the end of this chapter for some starting points. As you regularly and purposefully focus on all God is and all His power can accomplish in your life, you will begin to feel fear, anger and hopelessness melt away, making room for peace, clarity, and hope to fill your heart.

Key Learnings:

❤ While our heads may desire to be in God's presence, the access point for our heart is most often through praise.

❤ Our feelings don't dictate God's truth—His Word does.

❤ Praise is not an exercise in the power of positive thinking, but rather heartfelt statements of surrender to the sovereignty of God.

❤ The shortest route from panic to peace is through praise.

❤ "Worship while you wait." Worship helps us remember Who God is when answers to our prayers seem to be delayed or postponed.

❤ Worship requires sacrifice.

❤ Silence can be an act of worship.

❤ Worship, especially worship that draws on the truth and power of God's Word, is one of our greatest weapons against all of the enemies of our soul—the world, the flesh, and the devil.

Questions to Consider:

1. What role has worship played in your life?

2. What stands out for you as it relates to the power of worship?

3. How can worshiping while you wait for answers to your prayers bring you back to center?

4. How can you incorporate stillness into your worship of God?

5. What names/attributes from those listed below resonate the most with you?

6. How might they impact the way you engage in worship going forward?

Passages to Ponder:

As you reflect on these names and attributes of God, consider what Scripture says about the name of the Lord and how understanding its power forms the basis for our praise.

Proverbs 18:10, "The name of the Lord is a strong fortress; the godly run to him and are safe."

Psalm 5:11, "But let all those rejoice who put their trust in You; let them ever shout for joy, because You defend them; let those also who love Your name be joyful in You" (NKJV).

Stormie Omartian offers the following list of the names and Attributes of God[24]

He is Good (1 Chronicles 16:34)
He is Powerful (1 Corinthians 1:24)
He is Great (Psalm 86:10)
He is Excellent (Psalm 8:1)
He is Love (1John 4:6)
He is Wisdom (1 Corinthians 1:24)
He is Holy (Psalm 22:3-4)
He is Patient (Romans 15:5)
He is Changeless (Malachi 3:6)

He is Merciful (Psalm116:5)

He is Almighty (2 Corinthians 6:18)

He is Glorious (Exodus 15:11)

He is Righteous (Deuteronomy 32:4)

He is Just (Isaiah 45:21)

He is Grace (John 1:14)

He is Majestic (Isaiah 33:21)

He is All-Knowing (John 16:30)

He is All-Wise (Proverbs 3:19-20)

He is True (Jeremiah 10:10)

He is Pure (1John 3:3)

He is Sinless (1 Peter2:21-22)

He is Radiant (Hebrews 1:3 NIV)

He is Faithful (Deuteronomy 7:9)

He is Magnificent (Isaiah 28:29 NIV)

He is Worthy (Psalm 18:3)

He is my Creator (Psalm 139:13 TEV)

He is my Redeemer (Isaiah 59:20)

He is my Strength (Isaiah 12:2)

He is my Truth (John 14:6)

He is the Lifter of my Head (Psalm 3:3)

He is the All Sufficient One (2 Corinthians 12:9)

He is my Savior (Luke 1:47)

He is my Hope (Psalm 71:5)

He is the Son of God (Luke 1:35)

He is my Resurrection (John 11:25)

He is the Holy Spirit (Genesis 1:1-3)

He is the Light of the World (John 8:12)

He is the Lord of Lords (Deuteronomy 10:17)

He is the King of Kings (Revelation 17:14)

He is my Authority (Matthew 28:18)

He is My Consuming Fire (Deuteronomy 4:24)

He is my Restorer (Psalm 23:3)

He is my Comforter (John 14:15TLB)

He is my Stronghold in the Day of Trouble (Nahum 1:7)

He is my Resting Place (Jeremiah 50:6)

He is my Refiner (Malachi 3:2-3)
He is my Deliverer (Psalm 70:5)
He is my Refuge from the Storm (2 Samuel 22:3)
He is my Overcomer (John 16:33)
He is my Peace (Ephesians 2:14)
He is the Bread of Life (John 6:35)
He is my Fortress (Psalm 18:2)
He is my Everlasting Father (Isaiah 9:6)
He is my shade from the Heat (Isaiah 25:4)
He is my Healer (Malachi 4:2)
He is my Counselor (Psalm 16:7)
He is the Author of my Faith (Hebrews 12:2)
He is my Rewarder (Hebrews 11:6)
He is my Hiding Place (Psalm 32:7)
He is my Shield (Psalm 33:20)
He is my Purifier (Malachi 3:3)
He is my Sustainer (Psalm 55:22)
He is the Sovereign Lord (2 Samuel 7:28 NIV)

Prayer of Invitation:

Almighty God,
Praise You for Who You are and what You desire to do in and
through me. Please help me to better understand Your design
for worship and praise in my life. Show me how to make it part
of my lifestyle. I invite You to bring all that You are to bear on
my heart and the circumstances of my life. Help me break down
the barriers in my heart so that I can know the sweetness of an
intimate relationship with You. In the matchless name of Jesus,
Amen.

Practice Point:

Over the next month, select one name/attribute each day from the list provided by Stormie Omartian and speak words of thanksgiving and praise to God for Who He is and what He brings to your life.

Chapter Seven

The Strategic Heart: Living Out Your God Given Design

Personality tests and assessments abound, and many acknowledge the significant role our personalities play in the way we live out our day-to-day lives. Rarely, however, are our emotional needs or our spiritual personalities ever addressed; yet they both substantially influence the way we view God, how we desire to connect with Him and our response to His involvement in our lives. Understanding our personalities and in particular our emotional needs and spiritual personalities, contributes significantly to learning to live with our hearts at rest. A lack of self-awareness in this area is often at the core of some of our greatest sources of angst.

We all come with spiritual strengths and weaknesses that correspond to the way we are wired. Insights into our emotional needs and spiritual personalities often provide many "aha" moments as we respond to both the routine and radical events of our lives. It helps explain the *why* behind our thoughts, attitudes, and actions.

Several years ago, I received my certification as an Advanced Personality Trainer from CLASSeminars. (Christian Leaders, Authors, & Speakers) I can honestly say that the understanding I developed by engaging in the certification process has radically impacted my marriage, my parenting, my business and social interactions, and especially my walk with Christ. The freedom, grace, strength, and rest it has brought to my heart and my relationships is truly a gift.

I'd like to give credit to CLASSeminars and Florence Littauer in particular, for her expertise and influence in regard to the concepts discussed in this chapter.

To further grasp the significance of *your* heart and God's desire for you to live with it at rest, it is important to spend some time focusing on the uniqueness and intention with which you were designed. Your heart—that place where all the parts that make you *you* are integrated, including your personality, are designed by God, and are inextricably linked. Therefore, understanding our distinctive personality is not about labels or putting ourselves or others into a box. Rather, it is about recognizing the unique ways God hard-wired each one of us. As that clarity comes to settle in our minds and begins to form and inform new thoughts, attitudes, and actions, we experience that there is indeed a better way to live. Our hearts experience increasing measures of rest.

Christ had the strengths of each of the personalities but none of their weaknesses. Scripture provides examples of each of the personality types in action, helping us to see what they look like *with skin on*. For each of the four personality types that will be discussed (Sanguine, Melancholy, Choleric and Phlegmatic), we will touch on the unique ways that each personality type expresses the following: Visual Cues, Strengths, Weaknesses, and Emotional Needs. After surveying a few biblical examples, we will consider specific spiritual growth strategies that will facilitate our desire to live with our hearts at rest. A cursory look at each of these areas is all that can be addressed within the confines and context of this book. More information on each personality's Greatest Fears, Addictive Natures, Mechanisms of Control, Tips for Improved Communication, and Tempering Your Own Personality can be found in Appendix A. Should you wish to further investigate the personalities, I would highly recommend *"Wired That Way"* by Florence & Marita Littauer.

The personality name types for this particular model (*Wired That Way*) date back to the time of Hippocrates; hence the names are somewhat awkward. Adding some descriptors brings more clarity. **Popular** Sanguine (pronounced sang-gwin) is denoted by the color yellow, representative of their cheery disposition and bright outlook on life. In other personality models, sanguine closely resembles an otter type or is known as Fun Country. **Perfect** Melancholy does not mean folks with this personality type are perfect but rather that they are wired to bring structure and order. They are denoted by a navy-blue color, reflective of their more serious perspective on life. In other models, melancholies closely resemble the beaver type or are known to live in Perfect Country. **Powerful** Cholerics (pronounced collar ick) are denoted by the color red due to their flaming personality and authoritative presence. In other models, cholerics are known as a lion type or as someone who lives in Control Country. **Peaceful** Phlegmatics (pronounced fleg ma tic) are denoted by a forest green color, symbolizing their desire for and ability to bring peace. They are known in other models as the golden retriever type or someone who lives in Peace Country.

Keeping Our Personalities in Perspective

No one personality type is superior to another. You may feel more comfortable with certain personalities, but that doesn't make the others wrong, just different than yours. Each personality was created because each was needed to inherently provide something distinctive that does not come naturally to the other personality types. As you discover more about your own personality, you will see why you feel the way you do and learn strategies to better engage with those wired differently than you. When you understand what makes people tick, they are less likely to "tick you off."

Typically, no one is 100% one personality type to the exclusion of the others. Rather each person is a unique mix intentionally designed by God. This mix is usually comprised of a primary and secondary personality type sometimes sprinkled with learned behaviors from the other personality types.

Let this learning about your unique personality be an affirmation of the good work God has done and will continue to do in and through you. Let it be legitimizing and empowering. That was God's intention when He made you. This exploration into the personalities is intended to validate who you are and help you uncover God's very intentional design in and for your life. Ask God to help you see the value in the way He wired you. I spent years bemoaning my strong personality, seeing it to be a sort of curse that needed to be kept in check. My flaws and weaknesses seemed so evident, and I often felt misunderstood. Grasping God's design for me through studying these personalities has allowed me to see that He crafted my personality intentionally. He knew long before I was born what needed to be in my DNA to provide the support, advocacy, and tenacity my family would need. God does not make mistakes. If you're feeling like one, please ask Him to help you better understand His purposeful design for the deliberate way He made you.

Visual Indicators

Visual indicators are physical clues that reflect a person's personality. The clues include how a person is dressed, his or her posture, mannerisms, and facial expressions. Most people are unaware of how they "display" their personalities.

Popular Sanguines are loud and open. They have loud clothes with lots of bling and color. Their voices are loud; they use big wide gestures. For them, life is an open book, and they are often described as "touchy feely."

Perfect Melancholies are closed and quiet. They prefer to dress in subdued coordinating colors and are often seen wearing khakis with a very definite crease down the front. They keep their arm movements much closer to their bodies. They often speak softly and only when they feel it necessary.

Powerful Cholerics are forceful and functional. I believe they are the inventors of basic black when it comes to clothing. Everything about them—the way they dress, set up their desk, their car, or their home—is all about efficiency and functionality. Cholerics make life happen. They often walk and talk quickly. They carry a presence with them that is either energizing or intimidating.

Peaceful Phlegmatics are laid back and adaptable. They dress as casual as the situation will allow. They are quiet but witty, agreeable, and they make very good listeners. Phlegmatics can often be recognized by their posture. Their motto might well be, "why would you stand when you can sit and why would you sit when you can lie down?"

Common Strengths

Popular Sanguines are great starters and networkers. They make friends easily; they are energetic, optimistic, and enthusiastic. They charm, inspire, and cheerlead others and have the innate ability to bring lightness and brightness to their surroundings. They are often the rallying point for bringing people together.

Perfect Melancholies are organized, analytical, deep thinkers, and detail/schedule oriented. They love charts, graphs, and financial reports. They make friends cautiously but are deeply loyal to the ones they have. They will usually keep their work/living areas clean; in fact, their motto might be, "a place for everything and everything in its place."

Powerful Cholerics are natural-born leaders. They are decisive, independent, productive, goal-oriented, and resourceful. They multi-task with ease, and they excel in emergencies. They are able to quickly analyze a situation and determine which course of action is necessary to achieve the desired outcome.

Peaceful Phlegmatics are competent, easy-going, dependable, tolerant, and content. They are steady, even keeled and have lots of friends. They avoid conflict, are effective mediators, and function well in stressful situations.

As you look over the list of personality strengths, it's important to note that *any strength carried to an extreme becomes a weakness.*

Common Weaknesses

Popular Sanguines can be impulsive, forgetful, compulsive, and easily distracted. They often don't finish what they've started; they hate to work alone; they frequently interrupt others and find it easy to waste time.

Perfect Melancholies can be uptight, obsessive, critical, insecure, and skeptical. They can get stuck in planning mode and never get started on the actual project. Sometimes they are perceived to be depressed or "off in another world."

Powerful Cholerics can be bossy, impatient, and demanding of others. They tend to have little tolerance for mistakes and find it hard to apologize. They can run over people to achieve a goal and are prone to judge their value and the value of others on what they accomplish. They are notorious for being workaholics and focusing on the task instead of the person.

Peaceful Phlegmatics can be indecisive and hard to motivate. They typically avoid responsibility and find it difficult to take a stand. They tend to be sarcastic, judgmental, and compromising. They have a quiet will of iron and a propensity to laziness. Theirs are often sins of omission versus commission. It's what they don't do instead of what they do that is the issue.

If reading through these weaknesses has made you feel discouraged, maybe even disheartened, may I offer you some hope. First of all, recognizing our weaknesses is only part of the story. However, it is an important part. Knowing that the enemy of our souls will be lurking around us in our times of weakness, with the intent of sabotaging our lives, knowing our weaknesses is essential to defeating his plans and purposes for us.

Secondly, thank God for the transforming power of Christ and the gift of the Holy Spirit! That's what makes "a better way to live" possible. Just because our weaknesses exist, does not mean we have to live in them. As we let our weaknesses press us into a deeper relationship with our Heavenly Father, He will, by His Spirit, perform the ultimate renovation in our hearts. "Not by might; nor by power, but by Your Spirit" says the Lord (Zechariah 3:14).

I have prayed often that God would soften my heart, allow me to extend grace to myself and others and help me see people the way He does. As I've declared my dependency on Him to make the changes in my heart that I've been powerless to effect, I have seen Him do what only He can. He's changing my heart so that I am enabled to spend more time living in my strengths than in my weaknesses. As a result, I'm enjoying rest in my soul and greater delight in my relationships. I cannot always tell you how God works, but I can tell you that He does.

Emotional Needs

The emotional needs area often gets overlooked when trying to understand our God-designed wiring. It can even be discounted as unnecessary or too squishy. For those who dislike their emotions or find it difficult to talk about them, this conversation may seem akin to going to the dentist. Take heart, my friend; the truth is that God hard-wired us with these emotional needs *on purpose*. They are part of the deliberate individuality with which He crafted your heart. God knew what He was doing when He inserted them into your DNA. "Even though you may not be conscious that you even have emotional needs, those needs are at the core of your being. They are not just wants or desires; they are hard wired into who you are. And if those needs are not met in healthy ways, you will seek to have them met in other ways."[25] Emotional needs are not something to be ashamed of or something we can or should try to change. To be clear, our emotional needs are not an excuse for sinful behavior, and they need to be surrendered to Christ, as do all parts of our lives. Still, when you come to appreciate their significance, you begin to understand what motivates you, why some things matter to you and some things don't, as well as how and why you relate to others the way you do. It also helps to explain your greatest fears and your responses to others around you.

As you read some of the emotional needs for people with personalities quite different from yours, you may be tempted to think, *that's just an excuse or how can that be? Who really needs that?* May I gently remind you that those who are wired differently from you may be thinking the same thing about you and your emotional needs. When we engage with others whose personality is different than ours, we unintentionally withhold from them the very qualities they need from us. Because we don't have a particular emotional need, it doesn't even enter our minds that it could be a legitimate need for someone else. (This is especially true in marriages). For many people, grasping these concepts has allowed the proverbial "penny to drop" in their minds, bringing new awareness and grace to both themselves and their relationships. It has explained, and to a large degree resolved, the tension between my husband and me. Our relationship is much more tender and attentive now that I understand he doesn't intentionally try to do things (or not do things) that I find frustrating or hurtful. I've also learned that I can't expect him to naturally delight in meeting my "obvious" emotional needs because they aren't any more obvious to him than his are to me. It's made me more curious about his emotional needs and how to meet them and less focused on getting my own met.

Popular Sanguines

Attention. The loud voice, loud clothes, and attraction to bling (not just in clothes, but also in cars, home decor, gadgets, etc.) reveal how Sanguines are dying for us to notice their new outfit, new tech gadget, or whatever else will bring attention their way. They love to tell jokes and stories because then they have the attention of others. If they don't have your attention, they will go to great lengths to get it—even if it ends up not being positive attention they receive.

This behavior is observed in many rambunctious children in the classroom. Popular Sanguines want to be *popular,* and the effort they exert to try and make that happen extends well past the classroom into their adult years.

Affection. Sanguines love to give and receive hugs. They can stand so close beside you when they are talking to you that your personal space feels like it is being invaded. They are likely to put a hand on your shoulder or grab your arm in the midst of a conversation. Let me remind you that if you are not wired this way, you may find these actions frustrating, if not annoying. However, these are God-given hard-wired needs. Their actions are unconscious responses to the underlying need. If not met appropriately (by affection fitting to the nature of the relationship), they will look to unhealthy if not destructive ways to meet this need. Indeed, of all the personality types, this segment of the population is at the highest risk of inappropriate sexual behavior.

Approval. Popular Sanguines desperately want to be loved, and they want you to tell them so—often! Affirming them helps bring them back to center.

Fun & Adventure. A Sanguine's bubbly personality and positive approach to life is fueled by energy and excitement. Without it, they wither and wilt.

Perfect Melancholies

Sensitivity. Melancholy personalities are often misunderstood. These folks need to know people really care. They feel and care deeply about the individuals and experiences around them. Flippant words and dismissing attitudes are extremely hurtful to them.

Support. Melancholies need to know that you're "in their corner." Demonstrating an understanding of their circumstances goes a long way to providing the support they seek.

Space. From the melancholy perspective, hugs are not necessary when a handshake will do. Often, being left alone provides the processing/reflective space they need to bring an internal semblance of order to any chaos that may be occurring in their life.

Silence. Even without chaos, Melancholies crave the serene over the constant clutter and clamor of life. It allows them the chance to organize their thoughts and get things in order. Being bubbly and jovial in an attempt to cheer them up may have the opposite of its intended effect.

Powerful Cholerics

Sense of Control. Without at least a small sense of control, Cholerics feel trapped and undone. It is best to give them control of something, however small, or they will try and take control of everything.

Loyalty. Cholerics will go to the wall for those they lead/serve. In return, they are anticipating unwavering loyalty. If they don't receive it, they feel betrayed.

Credit for good work. Cholerics work hard with great stamina and fortitude, and their hard wired need is for others to acknowledge all their effort.

Achievement. Cholerics are born to accomplish. When they can't or don't, it is a source of much anxiety in their lives. Finding a place where they can effectively lead/accomplish helps restore their emotional balance.

Peaceful Phlegmatics

Peace and Quiet. Not unlike the perfect Melancholies, Phlegmatics enjoy solitude. It allows them to recharge, as they find being with people for extended periods of time to be very taxing.

Feelings of Self-worth. Feelings of inadequacy can be an area of struggle for Phlegmatics who are wired this way so regular, specific encouragement goes a long way to keep that in check. These folks need to know they are valued for who they are and not what they can do.

Respect. A Phlegmatic is laid back with an adaptable nature that can make them easy targets to be taken for granted. Phlegmatics need to know that their opinions and feelings matter, too.

Lack of Stress. Even though Phlegmatics are good under pressure, they are exhausted by it and often take great lengths to avoid it.

Biblical Examples/Spiritual Personalities

Popular Sanguine: Peter

Impulsive – Luke 24:12 "but Peter jumped to his feet…"

Loud – Acts 2:14 "Then Peter shouted"

Speaks without thinking – Matthew 26:69 after the denial of Jesus "he wept bitterly"

Spiritual strength – grace. Popular Sanguines often need a lot of grace, and they are quick to extend it to others.

Spiritual weakness – guilt. While Satan uses this tactic on all believers, guilt is particularly effective with this segment of the population.

Example of Christ – wedding in Cana

Perfect Melancholy: Moses

Uncomfortable in a crowd – Exodus 4:10 "I've never been good with words."

Fearful – Exodus 2:14, "people will know about this."

Humble – Numbers 12:3, "Now Moses was more humble than any other person on earth."

Good with details – Exodus 25-30 – specifications for building the Tabernacle

Spiritual Strength – Knowledge

Spiritual Weakness – value routine over relationship (can often focus on checking the box rather than connecting with God)

Example of Christ – going off alone to pray

Powerful Choleric: Paul

In your face – Galatians 2:11 – "I had to oppose him… for it was very wrong" (confrontation with Peter)

Hard worker - 1 Corinthians 15:10 – "Haven't I worked hard trying to do more than any of the others?"

Powerful – Acts 9:22 – "Paul's preaching become more and more powerful – no one could refute him" (he was right!)

Uncomfortable with display of emotion – Acts 21:13 – "Why all this weeping?" There was a job to be done!!!

Spiritual strength – justification – "I will show you my faith by my works" James 2:18

Spiritual Weakness – wrestle God for control

Example of Christ – clearing of the temple. In dealing with the Pharisees, Jesus "calls a spade a spade" - He KNEW He had the truth and they didn't. Christ furthered exhibited this personality type by all the miracles He was DOING.

Peaceful Phlegmatic: Abraham

Diplomatic – Genesis 18:23-33 – pleads for Sodom

Mediator – Genesis 13:7-9 "no need to fight – if you go left I'll go right; if you go right, I'll go left."

Compromising – Genesis 16:3 – takes Hagar as his wife to bear him a child even though God had promised to make him the father of many nations.

Spiritual strength – sovereignty of God

Spiritual weakness – complacency

Example of Christ – asleep in the boat, totally relaxed in God's ability to handle the situation

Spiritual Growth Strategies for each Personality Type

Popular Sanguine: A read-through-the-Bible-in-a-year schedule will not work well for you. You are likely to feel frustrated that you never made it past the middle of Genesis. Don't give up. Because that style doesn't work for you doesn't mean that you can't have a vibrant relationship with God. Become involved in a small group study for accountability, or perhaps you can organize or teach a study. Whatever shape it takes, participation is the key. Because stories (hearing them and telling them) are so much a part of their personality type, many Popular Sanguines find that supplementing their Bible reading with some Christian fiction has proven to be an effective tool for spiritual growth.

Perfect Melancholy: Many daily devotionals are created by writers with Melancholy personalities. While the material they present is valuable, it can often be lost by readers making sure that they don't miss a day or don't "check the box." Consider incorporating other activities into your quiet time that are not schedule-based, i.e. random, undated devotionals or readings. Learn to relax, allowing your ideals to be tempered with wisdom, knowledge, and compassion. Learn to be forgiving of yourself and others. Specifically ask God to show you the true meaning of grace and what He desires it to look like in your life. Seek a quiet place to meet with God, as distraction only breeds further frustration.

Powerful Choleric: You may want to get a prayer partner, as you may find larger groups too unfocused or inefficient. Still you will need to learn to be alone so that God has the time and opportunity to speak into your life. Use short devotional books with clear concepts that incite a call to action. Perhaps most importantly, set spiritual goals, not human goals. This will help you take the focus off of tasks and onto your personal growth and interaction with others. Specifically ask God to show you what it means for Him to be the Lover of your soul so you would learn/be able to receive His love and forgiveness.

Peaceful Phlegmatic: It will be important for you to make a commitment that is intentional but not legalistic. Pick the time that works best for you, and don't be in a hurry. You will want time to ponder. You might consider creating some traditions or rituals as anchoring points in your quiet time. For some people, listening to music or online devotionals helps foster a closer walk with God. You will need to vary your routine to prevent spiritual boredom, and, as with all personality types, comparison only leads to anxiety and a restless heart.

Satan Will Always Play to Your Weaknesses

We can never lose sight of the fact that while God desires for us to live in our strengths, knowing that when we do, our hearts will not only be at rest, they will also feel fully alive, the enemy of our soul has a primary and ultimate goal to steal, kill, and destroy. (John 10:10) I am not suggesting that we should live in fear of demons lurking at every corner, but to dismiss the enemy's influence in our fallen world and in our individual lives affords him a great advantage, as he is able to wreak untold havoc on our hearts and minds, virtually undetected. You may have heard of the expression of "kicking someone when they are down." The enemy is a master at that. When we find ourselves in difficult circumstances, he loves to plant seeds of doubt and fear in our minds that can blossom into all manner of scary feelings—panic, anxiety, rage, discouragement, and disillusionment, to name a few. He absolutely loves to draw our minds to potential places and scenarios that don't include God. When God is out of the picture, there is reason for fear, and Satan knows it. That is why he works so hard to play to our weaknesses. He knows in our own strength that we cannot resist the temptations he constantly throws our way. Whatever your personality weaknesses may be, you can count on him relentlessly tempting you to give into them and then making you feel guilty because you did.

As we read in John 4, Satan tried tempting Jesus, even though He had no weaknesses. He knew Jesus was sinless but he still tried to tempt him to sin. How much more will he barrage us with his tactics? Thanks be to God, Christ modeled a victorious response. Every time Satan proposed a new way for Christ to deny His Divine design, Jesus' answer was immediate and crystal clear, "It is written, it is written, it is written." He stood on the truth of Scripture and let its power come to bear on His circumstance. He demonstrated that inviting God, though His word, into His moment, gave Him the power He needed to prevail. God was honored and His heart was at rest.

Key Learnings:

❤ Your personality is an intentional gift to you and to the world from God.

❤ Your personality is never an excuse for sin.

❤ Any strength carried to an extreme becomes a weakness.

❤ When it comes to emotional needs, we often unintentionally withhold from those of other personality types the very things they need from us. Because we don't have that particular need, we assume they don't either.

❤ Satan will always play to your weaknesses.

❤ Christ always countered Satan's attacks with scripture.

Questions to Consider:

1. Based on your understanding of the personalities, identify your top 2 strengths.

2. Based on your understanding of the personalities, identify your top 2 weaknesses.

3. Knowing that any strength carried to an extreme becomes a weakness, can you identify any extremes in the way you do life?

4. How have you seen the spiritual strengths and weaknesses of your personality play out in your life?

5. Knowing that the enemy of our souls will always play to our weakness, what scriptures do you need to memorize and lean on to counter his attacks?

Passages to Ponder:

For Popular Sanguines (Fun Country):

"But He gives us more and more grace (power of the Holy Spirit, to meet this evil tendency and all others fully). That is why He says, God sets Himself against the proud and haughty, but gives grace [continually] to the lowly (those who are humble enough to receive it)" (James 4:6 AMP).

"Therefore, [there is] now no condemnation (no adjudging guilty of wrong) for those who are in Christ Jesus, who live [and] walk not after the dictates of the flesh, but after the dictates of the Spirit" (Romans 8:1 AMP).

For Perfect Melancholies (Perfect Country):

"Don't be impressed with your own wisdom. Instead, fear the LORD and turn away from evil" (Proverbs 3:7).

"What does the LORD your God ask of you but to fear the LORD your God, to walk in obedience to him, to love him, to serve the LORD your God with all your heart and with all your soul" (Deuteronomy 10:12 NIV).

For Powerful Cholerics (Control Country):

"Christ's love controls us. Since we believe that Christ died for all, we also believe that we have all died to our old life" (2 Corinthians 5:14).

"Submit yourselves, then, to God. Resist the devil, and he will flee from you. Come near to God and he will come near to you. Wash your hands, you sinners, and purify your hearts, you double-minded" (James 4:7-8 NIV).

For Peaceful Phlegmatics (Peace Country):

"For lack of discipline they will die, led astray by their own great folly" Proverbs 5:23 (NIV).

"If the godly give in to the wicked, it's like polluting a fountain or muddying a spring" (Proverbs 25:26).

Prayer of Invitation:

Lord Jesus,
Thank You for how You've wired me. Thank You that You made me with my unique personality for a purpose. Please show me how to live in my strengths and recognize the enemy's tactics when he's playing to my weaknesses. Guide me to the truths in Your word that I need to focus on when I'm struggling to be all that You intentionally designed me to be.

Practice Point:

Evaluate your current quiet time with the Lord, noting both its high and low points. Implement one of the spiritual growth strategies offered that corresponds with your particular personality for 21 days. Then re-evaluate your quiet time to see if there are new or improved levels of freshness and connection. Express your gratitude to God for how well He knows you and His attentiveness to your heart.

Chapter Eight

The Selfless Heart: Finding Freedom in Forgiveness

It's possible to be walking in obedience to Christ, engaging in meaningful spiritual disciplines, cultivating worship as our pattern of response, addressing our personality weaknesses, and still have a malaise over our heart. That feeling that something isn't quite as God intended it to be. That sense that freedom and wholeness are still just out of our reach. May I humbly suggest that unforgiveness could be at the root of those unresolved and disconcerting feelings.

As long as there are people on this planet, there will be a need for forgiveness—both extending it and receiving it. As I mentioned earlier, I love God, I'm just not crazy about all His people. The more years I spend in ministry, the truer that statement rings. Forgiving our brothers and sisters in Christ seems like it should be a given, but the truth is, it's often harder to forgive them because we think, *they should know better.* No matter who offends us or what their view of God might be, there is no shortage of opportunities in our life to extend forgiveness.

What is Forgiveness?

Simply stated, "to forgive someone means to let him off the hook or to cancel a debt he owes you."[26] That debt may be one of respect, personal safety, honesty, fidelity, gratitude, understanding, integrity. Add your circumstance to the list. In his book, *Landmines in the Path of the Believer*, Charles Stanley says, "We are to forgive so that we may enjoy God's goodness without feeling the weight of anger burning deep within our hearts."[27]

Forgiveness means releasing the offending party, leaving the event in God's hands, and moving on. Sounds so simple when you put it like that, but to travel the distance between theory and practice can seem an insurmountable feat at times. "To forgive means we will never get from that person what was owed us. And that is what we do not like, because that involves grieving for what will never be; the past will not be different."[28] If your past is marked by numerous hurts and deep wounds, there may be a lot of grieving still taking place in your heart and the very notion of forgiveness can seem torturous. Stormie Omartian reminds us that unforgiveness is even more tortuous. "If we don't forgive when we have been forgiven so much, we too will be locked up and tortured in our own soul. There is torture in not forgiving. Unforgiveness imprisons us. It shuts off the lines of communication between us and God. It makes us miserable. It's too easy to forget all that God has forgiven us and get petty with others. I am by no means suggesting that all unforgiveness is for petty reasons. Far too often the things that happen to us are serious and their impact and consequences are major. Forgiving at these times doesn't come easily or naturally."[29] But forgiveness is the *only* path to freedom. Praise God, Jesus' death on the cross not only to makes forgiveness possible, His resurrection provides the power we need to grant it to others. *He doesn't expect us to forgive others on our own, but He does expect us to forgive.*

Forgiveness is a Command in Scripture

Scripture does not suggest that we forgive, it commands that we do. While it remains our choice, God makes it clear in Scripture that if we want to move forward in our relationship with Him and live with our heart at rest, forgiveness is not optional. "You are God's chosen race, His saints; He loves you, and you should be clothed in sincere compassion, in kindness and humility, gentleness and patience. Bear with one another; forgive each other as soon as a quarrel begins. The Lord has forgiven you; now you *must* do the same" (Colossians 3:12-13)]Emphasis Mine] "Strong Words. They are so stark and direct, in fact, that we who are saved by grace yet unforgiving in our hearts find ourselves looking for loopholes, dodging the obvious, trying to convince ourselves that He must have meant something less exacting."[30] Yet, Scripture is crystal clear. "Let there be no more bitter resentment or anger, no more shouting or slander, and let there be no bad feeling of any kind among you. Be kind to each other, be compassionate. Be as ready to forgive others as God for Christ's sake has forgiven you" (Ephesians 4:31-32).

I cannot even begin to imagine some of the hard, harsh, and in some cases, downright horrific hurts that have happened to some of you who are reading these words. The concept of forgiveness may seem illusive at best, if not an entirely cruel prospect altogether. May I gently remind you once again, we must do the uncommon if we want uncommon results. "In dealing with hurtful, difficult situations in our lives, we must ask ourselves, *Is my ability or willingness to forgive another person based on the magnitude of the offense?* In other words, is there a threshold of pain beyond which we are not required to forgive—perhaps where it is *impossible* to forgive?"[31] The above passages and many others would say a resounding "no." It's important to remember that as your spirit and flesh wrestle through the deep weeds and wounds that make your heart heave at the very idea of forgiving, once again we cannot be led by our feelings. "You may not feel any natural great love toward the people who have brought such shipwreck into your life. No one would expect you to. But it will never be the depth of *your* love that causes you to forgive such heartless acts and attitudes. It will be—it can *only* be—the love of Christ transplanted into your believing heart and flowing through you to those who deserve it least." [32]

Who Am I Not Forgiving?

Many of us are familiar with the concept that forgiveness is an active decision. It is a choice we make. "We don't accidentally forgive someone without realizing it. But we certainly *are* able to *not* forgive someone without realizing it."[33] Read one woman's story,

> The first time I asked God if there was anyone I needed to forgive, it was because my Christian counselor, Mary Anne, was teaching me about the freedom and power of forgiveness. She had instructed me to forgive every person I needed to forgive so that nothing would stand in the way of all God had for me. I especially forgave my mentally-ill mother for being abusive to me when I was young. I had years and layers of not forgiving her to bring before God in order to be set free.
>
> The day I asked God about whether there was anyone else I needed to forgive, I did it more as a mere formality. Mary Anne told me she thought I needed to forgive my dad, but I didn't agree.
>
> "Forgive him for what?" I said, "He wasn't the abuser."
>
> "Just ask God about it. If there is anything there, He will tell you," she said, and she let it go at that.
>
> So I did ask God, thinking He would surely say, "There is absolutely no one you need to forgive, my good and faithful servant, but what a wonderful person you are to ask."
>
> I was wrong. Instantly I was struck through my heart with the truth. In that moment, I suddenly saw the whole picture. I had never forgiven my dad for not protecting me from my mother. And he was the only one who could. In all those years, my father had never rescued me from my mother's insanity, and I had held this against him without even realizing it.

That realization caused me to convulse with sobs, and I immediately confessed my lack of forgiveness toward my dad. I thanked God for releasing me from all the bitterness I had kept inside. When I did that, I felt a freedom and peace in my spirit like I had never known before. In retrospect, I believe that if I had not asked God to reveal any unforgiveness in my heart, I might never have seen this on my own.[34]

Before we explore the concept of forgiveness any further, may I ask you to stop reading, come before the Lord and ask Him if there is anyone in your life that you are unintentionally not forgiving. Give God time to break through any resistance your heart may be feeling. Worship Him as your Forgiver and Redeemer and ask Him to remind you of all that you have been forgiven.

Misconceptions About Forgiveness

We have faulty thinking when it comes to the concept of forgiveness and the enemy of our souls uses our flawed perspective repeatedly in our lives to impede the flow of God's grace and power. I invite you to join me in taking back any ground the enemy may have taken in your life by debunking the myths and exposing the truth.

Forgiveness is an act of denial. Many would say that by forgiving their offender, they are pretending that what was done to them never happened or that it really didn't cause any pain. That definition simply isn't true. The reason forgiveness is needed is because there was an actual offense committed. "You must name the sin against you to forgive it. God did not deny what we did to Him. He worked through it. He named it. He expressed His feelings about it. He cried and was angry. And then He let it go."[35]

Forgiveness is a sign of approval. Akin to the first misconception, there are those who would say that extending forgiveness to the person that hurt them is somehow saying that what was said or done to them was okay. Absolutely not. Forgiveness requires that something *wrong* has occurred in order for it to be necessary.

If I've truly forgiven someone, I won't ever have bad feelings about them again. "You may have genuinely trusted God to help you forgive your offender. But then the phone rings. Their birthday rolls around. A situation flares up where they handle a similar circumstance in the same insensitive way, and you feel your emotions start to heat up. That's when you might conclude, 'I guess I haven't really forgiven because if I had I wouldn't still feel this way.' But forgiveness cannot be proven by our feelings any more than it can be motivated or empowered by them. Forgiveness is a choice. And feelings often aren't. So it's quite possible to forgive someone the right way—God's way—and still have thoughts flash across your mind that seem to contradict the decision you made."[36] It's in those moments that you can worship God as your Forgiver and praise Him for the grace and power He offers you to live by faith and not by feelings.

Forgiveness means forgetting. The Bible never says that God *forgets* our sins, even though He has flung them "as far as the east is from the west" (Psalm 103:12). He simply has chosen not to remember them against us (Hebrews 10:17), not to bring them back up again, or to accuse and condemn us with them. Choosing not to remember isn't the same as forgetting. The fact that you have not been able to *forget* the offense doesn't necessarily mean you haven't *forgiven* it."[37]

"I'm sorry" equals forgiveness. The forced "I'm sorry" for the sake of fake peace is nothing more than fertile ground for resentment to grow. Forgiveness takes place in a repentant heart that takes ownership of the hurt they caused. Flippant words without taking personal responsibility or intending to change one's behavior reflects a proud and unrepentant heart. "They honor me with their lips but their hearts are far from Me" (Isaiah 29:13).

Forgiveness is a process. Nancy Leigh DeMoss, founder of Revive our Hearts Ministry, advocates that "there's no question that coming to grips with what can sometimes be an awful offense (or offenses) is often a long, arduous journey. But I've watched people 'working their way' toward forgiveness for years and years who simply never get there. In fact, I might go so far as to say that when forgiveness is seen as a work in progress, it seldom becomes a work in practice. By God's grace, you can choose to forgive in a moment of time—to the level of your understanding at that point. And though additional time and hard work may be required to live out the implications of that choice, the reality of being released from the prison cell of your own unforgiveness can happen today as an established fact. The choice for you to forgive is actually no more a slow-moving, wait-and-see process than God's forgiveness of you. Just as you were extended His grace in a moment of time, you can extend grace to others as a right-now expression of your will."[38]

True forgiveness requires reconciliation. We are wired to want our lives, our relationships, and our circumstances to continuously improve with an expectation of this is how it was meant to be. Living in a fallen world means that there are times when that ideal falls apart. It is during those times that some of us are wired to want to fix things, some to want resolution, some want everybody to be happy and others want to run from the conflict. Unfortunately, there are circumstances where none of these options are possible. That's because, "forgiveness takes one; reconciliation takes two."[39] "Not every offender is going to repent; not every relationship is going to improve."[40] Romans 12:18 instructs us that "as much as it depends on you, live at peace with all men." While we definitely have a part to play in the reconciliation process, there is clearly responsibility on the part of the offender in order for full reconciliation to take place. That you have no control of (or responsibility for). "Forgiveness has to do with the past. Reconciliation has to do with the future."[41]

Forgiveness is a guarantee against future hurts. To be sure, the challenging choice to forgive and the pain that precipitated it, can make our hearts want to recoil to avoid such difficulty in the future. Knowing our own propensity to *blow it* and sin's destructive effect on mankind as a whole, it would be naïve to think that such assurance is available. "As surely as you have been wronged in the past, you will continue to face situations where you will again be wronged, maligned and treated unfairly. Not even the power of forgiveness can prevent that from happening. To expect otherwise is to set ourselves up for disappointment and to live with the foul fruit of bitterness. That's why, if we are going to live at peace with God and our fellow man, forgiveness must be an ongoing way of life."[42]

Tell Tale Signs We Need to Extend Forgiveness:

Avoidance. Do you take steps to avoid seeing, talking to, or even thinking about people that have hurt or offended you? In extreme cases, avoidance might be the only safe alternative. However, more often than not, when we go out of our way to stay out of their way, it's because there are unresolved issues, and we'd rather avoid than address our need to forgive.

Angst at the mention of their name. Does something within you bristle when someone says their name? If so, you will not be able to suppress those feelings forever nor will they go away with time. They will just fester and unexpectedly splash out in sarcasm or scathing comments.

Anger. If the thought of the person makes your blood boil, or they can't even breathe without *ticking you off,* let those emotions be a clear indication that the flow of God's grace and power into your life has been severely hampered and immediate attention is required.

Reasons We Resist Offering Forgiveness

Pride. We like being the martyr, the one being wronged vs the one doing wrong. It's so easy to fall into the trap of gathering a following of people that sympathize with us over the wrong we have suffered. Our flesh loves the stroking it receives when others affirm us in the injustice we have endured. While support during or after a traumatic ordeal is completely appropriate, our human nature is often more willing to accept man's offer of *misery loves company* over God's offer of freedom through His redemptive power and grace. A cheap substitute indeed.

"When you refuse to forgive someone, you still want something from that person and even if it is revenge that you want, it keeps you tied to him forever."[43] Scripture provides a sober warning, "But if you refuse to forgive others, your Father will not forgive your sins" (Matthew 6:15). Knowing that truth and still refusing to forgive reveals an arrogance of spirit that God detests. "Rebellion is as sinful as witchcraft, and stubbornness as bad as worshiping idols" (1 Samuel 15:23).

Forgetting How Much You've Been Forgiven. We read in the story of the immoral woman who anoints Jesus' feet, that the Pharisees were indignant at her show of adoration and affection. Jesus' response is very telling. "Therefore I say to you, her sins, which are many, are forgiven, for she loved much; but he who is forgiven little, loves little" (Luke 7:47 AMP). The woman's understanding of her immorality sets her apart as one who has been forgiven much, enabling her to love Jesus with such passion and fervor. I'm wondering if it's because her sins were exposed that she actually realized how much she had been forgiven. Romans 3:23 says, "*All* have sinned and fall short of the glory of God (KJV) [Emphasis Mine]. Perhaps we would be more loving and more willing to forgive if our sins were exposed and we realized how much we have been forgiven. I believe it is spiritually very healthy to periodically ask God to show you your sin and allow you to feel the weight of it. Of course, we could not bear the full weight of it, but regular glimpses remind us of just how amazing grace really is.

Wrong thinking. We've all heard that adage that unforgiveness is like drinking poison and expecting the other person to die. We can be quick to dismiss that thinking as immature but our lives bear out what we truly believe. God in His providence does not allow any free passes when it comes to harboring bitterness and unforgiveness in our heart. "When you hold resentment toward another, you are bound to that person or condition by an emotional link that is stronger than steel. Forgiveness is the only way to dissolve that link and get free."[44] When we have been deeply hurt by someone, especially someone we love and trust, we somehow convince ourselves that our withholding of our forgiveness is going to *teach them a lesson*. The lesson we need to learn for ourselves is that while they may be experiencing freedom, we have forfeited our ability to do so. Even if the bond has been severed and there is no ongoing connection with that person, psychologist, Dr. Henry Cloud reminds us that "if I am not forgiving them, I am still in a destructive relationship with them."[45]

We haven't moved from woundedness to brokenness. If you remember back to chapter four, a wounded person is guarded, suspicious, fatalistic, bitter, easily angered, self-centered, are the walking wounded, have no evidence of the fruit of the Spirit, is self-sufficient, and harsh. Kind of sounds a lot like someone polluted by unforgiveness. There is a very direct correlation between woundedness and unforgiveness. Both are rooted in pride and focus on vindication and vengeance rather than forgiveness and freedom.

The Cost of Unforgiveness

While several of the costs for unforgiveness have already been mentioned, I would like to highlight a few more that leap off the pages of Scripture.

It deprives us and others of the grace of God. Forgiveness leads to life and peace while unforgiveness leads to death and misery. Our misery poisons those around us. "Be careful that no one is deprived of the grace of God and that no root of bitterness should begin to grow and make trouble; this can poison a whole community" (Hebrews 12:15). I wonder if we can truly comprehend how desperately we need God's grace and how much peace is robbed from our souls when we are deprived of it.

It affects our prayer life. "But when you are praying, first forgive anyone you are holding a grudge against, so that your Father in heaven will forgive your sins, too" (Mark 11:25). This passage makes it clear that holding a grudge is sin and known, unconfessed sin closes God's ear to the cries of His children. "If I had not confessed the sin in my heart, the Lord would not have listened" (Psalm 66:18). Folks, this is serious business.

If can affect our physical health. "When I refused to confess my sin, my body wasted away, and I groaned all day long. Day and night your hand of discipline was heavy on me. My strength evaporated like water in the summer heart" (Psalm 32:3,4). "Medical research has consistently shown that people who harbor pent-up emotions such as anger, bitterness, and inner hostility will often manifest these issues in their physical bodies. Such individuals frequently show a propensity for high blood pressure, impaired immune function, muscle spasms, hormonal changes, memory loss, even an increased risk of heart attack. Interestingly both the words *anger* and *angina* share the same Greek root."[46] Clearly not all our physical ailments and diseases are the result of unforgiveness. "I don't want anyone who suffers from organically rooted diseases to feel condemned or to suggest that you shouldn't pursue medical treatment for physical ailments. But I'm convinced that more often than we realize, some of the chronic, mental, emotional, and even physical disorders that people struggle with are rooted in anger we're unwilling to release. God never intended our bodies to hold up under the weight of unresolved conflict."[47]

It leads to a barrenness of soul. When we respond to the unjust and unkind happenings of our life like a debt collector, we fall back into woundedness and end up paying the bigger price. We develop the mindset that "until we get a satisfactory apology, until we determine that an adequate penalty has been paid, we reserve the right to keep him (her) in prison, to punish him for what he (she) has done."[48] As we read in Matthew 18:23-35, that plan is flawed.

"Therefore, the Kingdom of Heaven can be compared to a king who decided to bring his accounts up to date with servants who had borrowed money from him. In the process, one of his debtors was brought in who owed him millions of dollars. He couldn't pay, so his master ordered that he be sold—along with his wife, his children, and everything he owned—to pay the debt. But the man fell down before his master and begged him, 'Please, be patient with me, and I will pay it all.' Then his master was filled with pity for him, and he released him and forgave his debt. But when the man left the king, he went to a fellow servant who owed him a few thousand dollars. He grabbed him by the throat and demanded instant payment. His fellow servant fell down before him and begged for a little more time. 'Be patient with me, and I will pay it,' he pleaded. But his creditor wouldn't wait. He had the man arrested and put in prison until the debt could be paid in full. "When some of the other servants saw this, they were very upset. They went to the king and told him everything that had happened. Then the king called in the man he had forgiven and said, 'You evil servant! I forgave you that tremendous debt because you pleaded with me. Shouldn't you have mercy on your fellow servant, just as I had mercy on you?' Then the angry king sent the man to prison to be tortured until he had paid his entire debt. That's what my heavenly Father will do to you if you refuse to forgive your brothers and sisters from your heart."

Notice once again, the use of the words *prison* and *torture* in conjunction with unforgiveness. To demand payment from a fellow servant after he himself had been forgiven so much points to a hardness of heart and desolation of soul, that some might say deserve the harsh treatment the king invoked. The irony comes when we draw the parallel between how much we ourselves have been forgiven by our King and how eager we are to demand payment from our fellow brothers and sisters.

How Do I Forgive?

If you're like me, you may be convinced of your need to forgive and even have the desire to forgive but still lack clarity about how to put it into practice. Henry Cloud explains it this way, "Forgiveness is something we do in our hearts; we release them from the debt they owe us ... only one party is needed for forgiveness: me.... It is a work of grace in my heart."[49] Stormie Omartian offers this perspective, "Forgiveness is supernatural. Of course, you have to be *willing* to forgive, but in order to *truly* forgive, you need the Lord's enablement."[50] I believe the key is our willingness to forgive. The work of grace in my heart is reflected by my choice to forgive. As noted earlier, our feelings are not what authenticates forgiveness. Our heart-felt, intentional choice does. We may still battle with thoughts and feelings that are not congruent with our decision, but as always, Scripture has a remedy. Beth Moore calls this remedy, "re-wallpapering the walls of your mind."[51] Philippians 4:8 tells us to "Fix your thoughts on what is true and honorable and right. Thank about things that are pure and lovely and admirable. Think about things that are excellent and worthy of praise." Once again, I cannot stress strongly enough that this is not an exercise in the power of positive thinking but rather living in obedience to God's command to "take every thought captive" (2 Corinthians 10:5 NIV). Keep in mind that a step of faith always *precedes* the feelings of joy our hearts are looking for.

Forgiving Others

We've already talked a great deal about forgiving others, so I'd just like to share a brief story and then let Scripture speak for Itself. When my daughter was in junior high, she had a tiff with another girl at school. This kind of situation was uncommon for her so when she mentioned it, I asked her to tell me more about it. She gave a few brief highlights and then said, "I tried holding a grudge, but it was too much work." If we only understood how true those words are. We waste so much time and emotional energy when we refuse to forgive and choose instead to carry a grudge. Scripture is clear, "Never pay back evil for evil to anyone, Do things in such a way that everyone can see you are honorable. Do your part to live in peace with everyone, as much as possible. Dear friends, never avenge yourselves. Leave that to God. For it is written, 'I will take vengeance; I will repay those who deserve it,' says the Lord. Instead do what the Scriptures say: 'If your enemies are hungry, feed them. If they are thirsty, give them something to drink, and they will be ashamed of what they have done to you.' Don't let evil get the best of you, but conquer evil by doing good" (Romans 12:17-21). "Love prospers when a fault is forgiven, but dwelling on it separates close friends" (Proverbs 17:19). "But if you refuse to forgive others, your Father will not forgive your sins" (Matthew 6:15). "God's forgiveness is one of His greatest acts of love toward us. He wants forgiveness to be one of *our* greatest acts of love toward *others*."[52]

Forgiving God?

I have to admit that whenever I read about or hear someone speak in reference to the concept of forgiving God, something bristles within my spirit. The very essence of forgiveness requires that you are extending it because you were wronged. I understand the idea that we have to wrestle through tough times with God when we don't understand His sovereignty, and I would strongly advocate that you be very honest in those seasons of struggle. Ask Him, *Where are You? Where were You?* Tell Him, *You could have prevented this from happening. I feel like You abandoned me.*

Pour out your pain, describe your disillusionment with Him and His ways, absolutely. But to suggest that you, a mere mortal, need to forgive Almighty God is akin to blasphemy. May I remind you of God's response to Job after Job had vented His anger and despondency at the tragic happenings of his life. In Job 38 We hear God ask Job, "Who is this that questions my wisdom with such ignorant words? I have some questions for you and you must answer them. 'Where were you when I laid the foundations of the earth? Who defined the boundaries of the sea? Have you ever commanded the morning to appear and caused the dawn to rise in the east? (vs. 2, 4, 8, 12) God's challenge to Job continues for three more chapters until Job finally realizes the magnitude of the God he says he trusts ("though he slay me, yet will I trust in Him" Job 13:15 KJV) and the magnitude of his sin. He responds to the Lord in chapter 42 by saying, "You ask, 'Who is this that questions my wisdom with such ignorance?' It is I. And I was talking about things far too wonderful for me. I take back everything I said, and I sit in dust and ashes to show my repentance.'" (vs. 2, 3, 6) Job's sin is not in the wrestling, or the pouring out of his pain. It's in the shifting of his heart against God as revealed in the accusations he leveled against Him. "I cry to You oh God, but You don't answer me. I stand before You and You don't bother to look. You have become cruel toward me. You persecute me with Your great power." (Job 30:20, 21) Such statements reflect his pain for sure.

Unfortunately, they also reveal a heart that assumes his feelings dictate truth, completely dismissing the heart and sovereignty of God, Who is supreme over *all* creation.

Notice that it was after Job was reminded of God's character and power (albeit in a very dramatic conversation with Almighty God Himself!) that he recognized the error of his ways and his way of thinking. When we lose our sense of awe before God, we lose perspective. Praise has power to not only change our viewpoint, but also to turn our heart back to God. And the way back my friends, is through repentance—us asking God for forgiveness. "Now turn from your sins and turn to God, so you can be cleansed of your sins. Then wonderful times of refreshment will come from the presence of the Lord" (Acts 3:19, 20).

Forgiving Yourself

Romans 8:1 tells us, "So now there is no condemnation for those who belong to Christ Jesus." Our heads know this truth, but our hearts have trouble buying into the idea. Why is that? I believe there are two main reasons.

We are believing the lies of the enemy.

We are letting our hearts lead our heads.

Either way, we are led to paralyzing guilt and robbed of all God intended to do in us, through us and for us. "As Philip Yancey points out, 'Guilt is not a state to cultivate or a mood you slip into for a few days. It should have directional movement, first pointing backward to the sin and then pointing forward to change. A person who feels no guilt can never find healing. Yet neither can a person who wallows in guilt. The sense of guilt only serves its designed purpose as a symptom if it presses us toward a cure.'"[53] Hebrews 10:19, 21, 22 reminds us of the ultimate cure that definitively declares victory over our guilty conscience, "And so, Dear brothers and sisters, we can boldly enter heaven's Most Holy Place because of the blood of Jesus … And since we have a great High Priest who rules over God's people, let us go right into the presence of God, with true hearts fully trusting Him. For our evil consciences have been sprinkled with Christ's blood to make us clean, and our bodies have been washed with pure water."

It is Written

Christ gives us a powerful model of how to deal with the lies of the enemy in Matthew chapter four, where we read of His temptation in the desert. Christ's response to every lie (disguised as an opportunity or a shortcut!) the enemy threw at Him was, "It is written. It is written. It is written." (vs. 4, 7, 10 KJV) Our response to the lies the enemy throws at us should be the same. Here are just a few of his common lies and Scripture's bullets of truth.

I need to be perfect. "The Lord is like a father to His children, tender and compassionate to those who fear Him. For He understands how weak we are; He knows we are only dust" (Psalm 103:13, 14). Any expectation of perfection, does not come from God.

My sin is too great. God may be able to forgive me for some things, but not this. "If we confess our sins, He is faithful and just to forgive us our sins and to cleanse us from *all* unrighteousness" (1 John 1:9 KJV) [Emphasis Mine].

God is disappointed in who I am. This lie suffocated my heart for many years. Zephaniah 3:17 says otherwise, "For the Lord your God has arrived to live among you. (He *wants* to be with me) He is a mighty Savior. (He brings His power into my life). He will rejoice over you with great gladness. (I really can bring Him joy). With His love, He will calm all your fears. (He knows my fears and cares enough to want to calm them) He will exult over you by singing a happy song." (I can actually live in a way that makes Him proud of me.)

There are other lies that the enemy will use to try to discourage, defeat, or distract us, so I encourage you to regularly ask God, "what lies am I believing?" Then ask Him to show the truth in His Word. Ask Him also to attune your ear to His voice of truth so that you better recognize the lies of the enemy. After that, ask yourself,

"Am I cheapening the price Christ paid for my sin by refusing to receive the forgiveness He offers?"

The Daily Gospel

This last question may seem quite harsh, but it is often the point where many people stumble and get stuck in their walk with Christ. We understand the value of asking for forgiveness and receiving it by faith at the time of our conversion to Christ but fail to see that daily confession, repentance, and forgiveness are necessary to address the ongoing sin in our lives. We don't need to come to Christ to ensure our eternal salvation on a daily basis, but we do need to deal with our sin every day. The sense of unresolved guilt in our hearts is often the result of unconfessed sin. Sometimes, it is blatant sin we're intentionally trying to hide from God. Other times, it's an unarticulated haze over our hearts that we can't quite put our finger on. King David could relate. "How can I know all the sins lurking in my heart? Cleanse me from these hidden faults. Keep me from deliberate sins! Don't let them control me. Then I will be free of guilt and innocent of great sin" (Psalm 19:14).

The message of the Gospel is only good news if we receive it by faith. "The just shall live by faith" (Romans 1:17 KJV). "Without faith it is impossible to please God ..." (Hebrews 11:6). That is true in our daily 'confessing and repenting' lives as well. We must come before the Lord each day, confessing our sin, repenting of it and asking for His forgiveness. Then we must *choose* to receive it by faith. Our hearts may not always *feel* forgiven but God's Word says they are. (1 John 3:20-22 NIV)

I've started a new practice that has really helped me to lead my heart when it struggles to *feel* forgiven. When I confess my sin to God, I thank Him for His love and forgiveness. I tell Him that I choose to receive it by faith and then I ask Him to let the power of His love and forgiveness change me. It has!

Key Learnings:

- Forgiveness is a command not a suggestion in Scripture.
- Forgiveness is not a process.
- We often resist offering forgiveness because we prefer to play the martyr.
- God in His providence does not allow any free passes when it comes to harboring bitterness and unforgiveness in our heart.
- If I am not forgiving someone, I am still in a destructive relationship with them.
- The work of God's grace in my heart is reflected by my choice to forgive.
- The sense of unresolved guilt in our hearts is often the result of unconfessed sin.

Questions to Consider:

1. Which of the misconceptions about forgiveness was exposed for you today?

2. Do you recognize any "Tell Tale Signs" of unforgiveness?

3. What reason for resisting forgiveness do you resonate with most?

4. How do you keep from forgetting how much you've been forgiven?

5. Are there costs you are paying for unforgiveness? What are they?

6. How would you describe your response to Job's interaction with God?

7. Has God revealed any unforgiveness in your heart? Are you willing to forgive?

Passages to Ponder:

"They refused to obey and did not remember the miracles you had done for them. Instead, they became stubborn and appointed a leader to take them back to their slavery in Egypt! But you are a God of forgiveness, gracious and merciful, slow to become angry, and rich in unfailing love" (Nehemiah 9:17).

"For the honor of your name, O Lord, forgive my many, many sins" (Psalm 25:11).

"Though we are overwhelmed by our sins, you forgive them all" (Psalm 65:3).

"I will cleanse them of their sins against me and forgive all their sins of rebellion" (Jeremiah 33:8).

"Oh, what joy for those whose disobedience is forgiven, whose sins are put out of sight" (Romans 4:7).

"But if we confess our sins to him, he is faithful and just to forgive us our sins and to cleanse us from all wickedness" (1 John 1:9).

"Yes, this anguish was good for me, for you have rescued me from death and forgiven all my sins" (Isaiah 38:17).

In addition to these passages, flip back through the chapter to find a passage that really resonated in your heart. Spend some extra time ruminating on it, letting it soak into your soul.

Prayer of Invitation:

Lord Jesus,

Help me break free of any prison of unforgiveness I have created for myself. Grant me the resolve to extend forgiveness to myself and to those You bring to my mind. I know that I cannot do this on my own, so I'm inviting Your power to work through me. May my understanding of the depth of the forgiveness You've offered me propel me to offer it to those who have hurt me. Expose the lies the enemy wants me to believe and show me how to live by faith and not by feelings. In the mighty name of Jesus, I pray, Amen.

Practice Point:

Like forgiveness, laundry is something we get to do regularly, even if we don't feel like it. The next time you are sorting clothes for the wash, let it remind you of the filth that sin has brought into your heart and life. As you put the clothes in the washing machine, allow the action to serve as an analogy of our dependence on Christ as the only one Who can remove the stench and stain of sin.

When you bring clothes out of the dryer, inhale deeply as you breathe in the fragrance of forgiveness.

Chapter Nine

The Secure Heart: Finding Financial Peace in a Debt-Crazed World

"I will both lie down in peace, and sleep; for You alone, O Lord, make me dwell in safety" (Psalm 4:8). This verse can seem like a pipe dream when both peace and sleep elude you in the lonely hours of a long night of persistent stewing over your financial situation. I know because I have some pretty solid experience in trying to wrestle down the anxious thoughts that caused my heart to rev with nervous tension. There was a time when I would have considered myself a master strategist in financial gymnastics, as I turned myself inside out trying to stretch our income to match our outflow. While my husband and I have made our share of financial mistakes, neither of us are big spenders. We each grew up in modest homes, where spending was focused on the essentials. Extras were a luxury. I mentioned earlier that I often heard these words throughout my childhood, "We can't afford it, we can't afford it, we can't afford it." The seeds of insecurity those words planted in me, grew into a full-blown lack mentality which did not leave me in adulthood. In fact, I believe it grew stronger as I let my self-esteem become entangled with my financial circumstances. I began to feel "less than" when my husband and I struggled to pay the bills. I'd lay awake at nights and stress during the day to construct the financial strategies necessary to keep the bases covered. The thought of not having enough money to pay a bill simply undid me. To compound the situation, I had no training in the area of finance or investments so, at times, I felt financially incompetent and just plain stupid. My parents couldn't teach me what they hadn't been taught themselves, but they taught me very clearly the importance of keeping your bills paid. They also taught me the value of family and that money isn't everything. I've never aspired to being rich and I can honestly say that getting the biggest, brightest, best or newest has not been something my soul has had to contend with. However, the fear of not having enough has plunged me into panic on many occasions.

The values ingrained in me by my parents were easier to embrace when we went to Bible College as married students. (I already had my undergrad degree so I worked at the college while my husband pursued his degree.) Within the married student community, no one had any money so not having any didn't seem shameful or embarrassing. It was normal. Popcorn and a rented (or borrowed) movie at a friend's house was our version of a night out. Those days were a pleasant reprieve from having to wear the money masquerade mask. You know the mask you wear when you feel compelled to let on that you have more money than you really do. The mask that keeps you from saying, "I'm sorry, I can't afford that right now."

Coming out of that culture and into mainstream materialism was challenging. As I said earlier, I never have been a big spender or a shopaholic. Even today, I don't really enjoy shopping. I'm much more of a make a list, get the list, and get-on-with-your-day kind of person. Still, the world's values around money can leave you feeling devalued. Why does it have such an effect on us? What is it about our money (or lack of it) that is such a source of insecurity for us? I believe it is a heart issue that is normally neglected but needs to be resolved. I also firmly believe that there is no way we can live with our hearts at rest until we make room for God in our finances.

Why do our Finances Matter to God?

They're part of our heart so they matter to God. Our hearts really do matter to God. All the parts of our heart, not just the ones we consider to be more *spiritual* than others. Money is a spiritual matter and often serves as a telltale barometer for our heart's spiritual health. In fact, in Scripture, God speaks more about money than almost any other subject. He knows it's a big deal. Additionally, His favor includes (but certainly is not limited to) financial blessings.

Contrary to what some would believe, God is not against His people having large sums of money. Many godly characters in the Bible had significant amounts of wealth. Other equally godly people had very little money. It's not about the amount of money we have or don't have. The issue surfaces and then takes root when our focus on money gets a disproportionate place in our hearts and we develop a misplaced sense of security. "For where your treasure is, there your heart will be also" (Matthew 6:21 NIV). Money expert, Dave Ramsey reminds us that, "When we forget that our money is not our Creator—that instead we are supposed to create with it—we wreak havoc in our lives."[54] Exodus 34:14 states God's position plainly, "You must worship no other gods, for the LORD, whose very name is Jealous, is a God who is jealous about His relationship with you." *He wants first place in our hearts and giving that to anyone or anything else will always cause anxiety to rise up within us.*

He knows how finances cause us stress. God has always known that money would be part of our lives and stewarding it well would be part of our struggle. 1 Timothy 6:10 tells us that "the love of money is the root of all kinds of evil." He understands that when anything or anyone but Himself occupies that place in our heart reserved for Him alone, things will be off kilter and we will experience angst in our spirit. That is true whether we have a lack mentality or struggle with greed. He also understands this is when we become spiritually vulnerable and are prone to make poor choices. Clearly, not all financially difficult circumstances are the result of poor choices, but God can use financial pressure, however it comes, as a way of getting our attention and refocusing our heart.

God is not being cruel when He allows difficult financial circumstances in our lives. Rather He uses such circumstances as an effective tool in recalibrating our hearts and as a platform for Him to demonstrate His care for us. 1 Peter 5:7 invites us to "cast our cares on Him because He cares for us." His invitation includes our finances. "If your earthly father knows how to give good gifts, how much more will your Heavenly Father give to those who love Him?" (Matthew 7:11). I wonder how often we forfeit His peace and provision because we choose to not rely on Him, struggling instead to figure it out on our own. Choosing to trust God is always a deliberate choice and the degree to which we trust God will be the degree to which we experience rest for our souls. We need to be intentional about trusting God with our finances, especially when there's not enough money to go around. His Word provides the perspective we need to lean in deeply. "And if God cares so wonderfully for wildflowers that are here today and thrown into the fire tomorrow, he will certainly care for you. Why do you have so little faith? So don't worry about these things, saying, 'What will we eat? What will we drink? What will we wear?' These things dominate the thoughts of unbelievers, but your heavenly Father already knows all your needs. Seek the Kingdom of God above all else, and live righteously, and he will give you everything you need" (Matthew 6:33).

I remember during our early years of marriage watching friends we knew, who didn't have much money, regularly receive financial gifts from unforeseen sources. Money would come unexpectedly in the mail, sometimes with no indication of who it was from. People would give them furniture or appliances, provide repair services for free, offer them free use of their recreational toys. While I was happy for these friends, as I knew they needed the help, I have to be honest. There were times when I thought, *Why doesn't this ever happen to us?* My husband and I had only been married a couple of years at that time and even though we were both working full time, money was tight. Neither of us came from families of means so we needed to make our own way in the world. I was still paying off a student loan and being married young meant we had no financial reserves to draw from. I recall a sense of *God, don't You see how hard we're working, too? What about us?* I compared our need to theirs and sometimes it felt like ours was greater. *In all areas of our lives, including our finances, comparison will steal our joy and rob our peace.*

A number of years later, we found ourselves in an unanticipated season of financial strain. I had recently been diagnosed with Rheumatoid Arthritis and its onset had been very aggressive so I was unable to work or care for our then four-year-old son (who has Cerebral Palsy) for about three months. My husband suffered a work related back injury during that time so he was off work and only receiving a fraction of his regular salary. Christmas was approaching, and it was clear that if we stretched our pennies, we might be able to cover our mortgage payment and utility bills, but there would certainly not be anything available for Christmas gifts or the typical seasonal festivities. One day, as my husband and I sat on the couch discussing how best to navigate the difficult days ahead, our doorbell rang. A group of people from our church came to deliver a very timely reminder that God does see our need, and He is able to provide in abundance! Not only were there gifts for each of us, including a hand knitted throw blanket for me, but a sizable cash gift that eased some of the financial squeeze we were experiencing. It was a very humbling incident in our lives for sure, but also a very tangible reminder of the promise of God's Word, "My God shall supply all your needs, according to His riches in glory" (Philippians 4:19 KJV).

Contentment reflects a trusting heart. "Yet true religion with contentment is great wealth. After all, we didn't bring anything with us when we came into the world, and we certainly cannot carry anything with us when we die. So if we have enough food and clothing, let us be content. But people who long to be rich fall into temptation and are trapped by many foolish and harmful desires that plunge them into ruin and destruction" (1 Timothy 6:6-9). We've all been confronted by the 'big green monster' of envy at some point in our lives. In Ecclesiastes 4:4, King Solomon, "observed that most people are motivated to success because they envy their neighbors. But this, too, is meaningless—like chasing the wind." Proverbs 14:30 teaches us that "A heart at peace gives life to the body, but envy rots the bones." The reason it rots our bones is because our focus is squarely on our perceived lack, and we carry the weight of trying to find a way to make up what we feel is missing. As always, Jesus modelled a better way to live. "When Jesus saw the need to feed 5000 people, He took five loaves of bread and two small fish and *gave thanks to God for it* (John 6:11-13). If Jesus gave thanks to God before seeing what He had multiplied, how much more should we do the same? Giving thanks and praise to God for what we have increases it to become something greater than it is. *There is a principle here that is worth repeating. Jesus gave thanks for what He had, and God multiplied it to what He needed."*[55] Contentment reflects that shift in the posture of our heart that demonstrates that we do, indeed, trust in His provision. Admittedly, contentment can be very difficult when you can clearly see your need and God's provision has yet to come into view. This is yet another example of what Scripture means when it says, "we live by faith and not by sight (2 Corinthians 5:7 NIV). This is where we get to live the way we say we believe.

Guidelines for Giving

Give to God. "One-tenth of the produce of the land, whether grain from the fields or fruit from the trees, belongs to the Lord and must be set apart to him as holy" (Leviticus 27:30).

Give to the government. Then Jesus said to them, "Give to Caesar what belongs to Caesar and to God what belongs to God" (Mark 12:17).

Give to yourself (savings). "The wise have wealth and luxury, but fools spend whatever they get" (Proverbs 21:20).

Live on the rest. (note the word rest) "Yet true godliness with contentment is itself great wealth" (1 Timothy 6:6). "Just as the rich rule the poor, so the borrower is servant to the lender" (Proverbs 22:7). Living within your means is uncommon in our debt-crazed world. But friends, that is God's heart for us. He knows that is the only avenue to peace. There are no shortcuts.

Give generously. As God enables you, give to others. It doesn't always have to be money. It can be your time, your talents, or items you give to others rather than sell. However, something happens in us when we share money with others. Dave Ramsey observes, "I do not totally understand what giving does to the human spirit, but I do know that I meet very few well-balanced, happy, healthy, wealthy people who don't give money away."[56] "God loves a cheerful giver" (2 Corinthians 9:7).

Why Tithe?

It is a step of obedience. "A tithe of everything from the land, whether grain from the soil or fruit from the trees, belongs to the Lord; it is holy to the Lord" (Leviticus 27:30). "Be sure to set aside a tenth of all that your fields produce each year" (Deuteronomy 14:22).

Tithing is a significant way in which we demonstrate our faith in God's provision. "And this same God who takes care of me will supply all your needs from his glorious riches, which have been given to us in Christ Jesus" (Philippians 4:19). However, it's not about giving to God so that He now "owes you." He is no man's debtor. It's about deciding to make room for Him in our finances, no matter what.

God's provision is not limited to money. Some of His provision comes through our possessions not breaking down. A car or an appliance that keeps faithfully working can be just as much an act of His care as a surprise envelope in the mail. His care and provision might look like a pair of gently used soccer shoes or hockey skates handed down by a neighbor or family member in a season when your child's feet are growing at a rapid pace. Purchasing good quality items at garage sales or through online buy and sell websites can be a way to trim some expenses out of your budget. For those of you who resist buying anything that is not brand new, may I remind you that every time you sleep at a hotel, you are paying to sleep on a used mattress.

It is a discipline that helps us live expectantly rather than entitled. Note it is a discipline and "No discipline seems pleasant at the time, but painful. Later on, however, it produces a harvest of righteousness and peace for those who have been trained by it" (Hebrews 12:11). It may be tempting to think of what you could buy with your tithe money instead of giving it to God but I have yet to meet anyone who has found that to be a beneficial decision. As we see from the above verse, God promises that He will honor our choice to honor Him by granting us peace. Not until we don't have it do we understand the value of financial peace. Submitting to His training in this area of our lives demonstrates the shift from an entitled posture of "I deserve it" to an expectant posture of "Thank You for Your promise to provide."

It helps us recognize the Source of our earning power. "Whatever is good and perfect comes down to us from God our Father, who created all the lights in the heavens. He never changes or casts a shifting shadow" (James 1:17). "Who am I, and who are my people, that we could give anything to You? Everything we have has come from You and we give You only what You first gave us!" (1 Chronicles 29:14). Enough said.

It is an act of worship. "Honor the Lord with your wealth and with the first fruits of all your produce" (Proverbs 3:9). As was mentioned earlier, money is a very spiritual matter. We live out the faith we say we have and the love we profess to have for God when we give Him access to our wallets.

It guards our hearts. Many of us leave our hearts unguarded in this area and suffer anxious days and sleepless nights as a result. As I noted in chapter one, guarding our heart is not just about what we protect it from; it's also what we put in it to fortify it. Living in obedience to God's ways with our finances does an anchoring work in our hearts that reinforces our trust in His character and power. Undeniably, honoring God with our money will not always be easy, nor will we always know the best way to do it. Faithfully, God's Word provides the guidance we need. "Don't worry about anything; instead, pray about everything. Tell God what you need, and thank Him for all he has done. Then you will experience God's peace, which exceeds anything we can understand. His peace will guard your hearts and minds as you live in Christ Jesus" (Philippians 4:6,7).

The Cost of Disobedience with Our Finances

We are robbing God and cannot experience His full blessing in our lives. "Will a mere mortal rob God? Yet you rob me. But you ask, 'How are we robbing you?' 'In tithes and offerings…. bring the whole tithe into the storehouse, that there may be food in my house. Test me in this,' says the Lord Almighty, 'and see if I will not throw open the floodgates of heaven and pour out so much blessing that there will not be room enough to store it.'" (Malachi 3:8,10). Obedience brings blessing. There simply is no other way.

We settle for second best. When we rush ahead of God to gain more stuff, we lose out on His plan for us in that particular circumstance, including experiencing His care for our hearts. When we make purchases on our credit card for items we cannot afford to pay for with cash or regularly borrow from family and friends to provide for our needs, we are taking away the opportunity to experience God's supernatural provision for us. When we become excessively stressed and plunge into financial panic mode, we become predisposed to knee-jerk reactions and a self-sufficient sense of *if it's going to be, it's up to me* rises up within us. God's promptings of direction and whispers of comfort fall on deaf ears and then we feel victimized by His lack of concern or intervention in our circumstances. Is it possible that if you're wondering why you have never received any unexpected provision from God, it's because you have a habit of already deciding that your way is better than His? You rush in with your plans even before you know what His are? Then you accuse Him of not caring. That is definitely not God's best or His heart for you. He had a better way, but you chose second best.

I can guarantee you that God's plans will take longer to unfold than your heart has patience for, but hear the words of warning He gave to the Israelites, "Only in returning to me and waiting for me will you be saved. In quietness and confidence (trust) is your strength. But you would have none of it. You said, 'No, we will get our help from Egypt. They will give us swift horses for riding into battle'. But the only swiftness you are going to see is the swiftness of your enemies chasing you!" (Isaiah 30:15,16). Through the years, I have felt the swiftness of financial pressure chasing me enough times to know there must be a better way to live and there is. Here are a few practical tips:

Practical Tips

Develop a budget. It's actually freeing versus restrictive. It's not about what you're saying no to; it's what you're saying yes to. Dave Ramsey can often be heard saying, "If you don't tell your money what to do, it will tell you what to do." Many people know only too well the pain of their money (or lack of it) telling them what to do (or what they can't do). Knowing where your money is going each month restores a sense of control and goes a long way to quieting the chaos in your soul. It also provides the peace of knowing you're stewarding well all that God has given you. There are a plethora of online resources available to help you set up a simple but effective budget.

Avoid debt at all costs. Debt chokes your future. Do not sacrifice or sabotage all God has for your future by thinking you have to have it all now. Jeremiah 29:11 tells of the plans God has in mind for you, "plans for good and not for disaster, to give you a future and a hope." There is nothing good about large amounts of personal debt. It can lead to disaster. It steals your future and robs your hope.

Living within your means and with reasonable debt (i.e. a mortgage) is definitely not common in our North American society. In order to live this way, you will not be able to have everything you want or that your friends have. But you will also have something they don't—freedom from the stranglehold of debt. "The blessing of the Lord makes one rich and He adds no sorrow with it" (Proverbs 10:22). Debt is a big sorrow.

Save for the future. I noted this idea in "Guidelines for Giving" but it bears repeating. "Give portions to seven, yes to eight, for you do not know what disaster may come upon the land" (Ecclesiastes 11:2). I am not suggesting you live in fear of impending doom but having some funds in reserve makes the inevitable unexpected happenings of life less taxing.

Get outside help if necessary. Sometimes we don't know what we don't know. That was certainly the case for me. Budgeting, investing, and financial planning are all skills I knew I didn't know enough about, so I searched for people who could help me learn what I needed to know. Don't feel ashamed. Others only know what they know because somebody taught them.

Build in accountability. Managing our money (and our spending) in a way that honors God is not always easy. It is definitely a case of doing the uncommon in order to achieve uncommon results. Invite a trusted person to keep you accountable and encourage you along the way.

Plan your meals in advance. It is never a good idea to shop when you're hungry and leaving meal planning to the last minute often leads to disaster. Also, you spend differently when you're in a hurry. I have used a "Once a Month" meal planning program for many years now. It was especially helpful when our children were at home. I spent less on groceries and it alleviated the dreaded question, "What's for dinner?"

Shop with a list and for a purpose. A list helps you remember what you need but also tells you what you don't need. Unless it's a glaring oversight, leave it out of your cart. Rarely does anything good come from window shopping at the mall. More than likely, the large selection will taunt you with what you don't have and plant seeds of discontent and envy in your heart. When we were at college, I had a friend who said, 'I don't look at the flyers that come in the mail any more. They just make me want what I can't afford.'

God desires financial peace for us. He wants our focus to be on Him and His calling on our life. Finances will always be a necessary part of our lives but they don't have to consume such disproportionate amounts of our physical, mental, emotional, and spiritual energy. Our Heavenly Father dearly wants our hearts to be at rest but rest can't happen until we invite Him into our finances and live, give, spend, and save the way He teaches us to in Scripture. When that shift in the posture of our heart takes place, these truths all start to make sense and our new found understanding gives birth to a fresh sense of motivation to steward our finances in a way that honors God. Until then, the financial battle will seem confusing. You will feel the bristle of resistance in your heart. Pray that God would bring clarity to you (and your spouse if you have one) and change your *want to* where necessary.

Let me close this chapter with a poignant reminder of why we don't want to spend large quantities of our life focused on finances. I sat, over a cup of hot tea, listening to a woman who has, through the years, both formally and informally, served as my mentor. She and her sister had recently finished the unenviable task of cleaning out the room in a retirement home that had belonged to their recently departed mother. Amongst the sorrow she felt at the loss of her mother, she was musing at the disconcerting reality that, after the furniture had been hauled out of the care facility and her clothes given to charity, her mother's entire life of ninety plus years had been reduced to just a few boxes. All those years, condensed to so little. How could a handful of cardboard boxes tell the real story of her life?

Friends, all too soon, our loved ones will be sorting through our things and putting some of them in boxes as keepsakes. May what they put in those boxes be lifelong reminders to them of how much you loved Jesus and how your actions demonstrated that His way is always best and that He is worth trusting no matter what.

Key Learnings:

- 💙 Tithing is a significant way to demonstrate our faith in God's provision.
- 💙 Guidelines for Giving. Give to God; give to the government, give to yourself (savings), and live on the rest. As God enables, give to others.
- 💙 When we rush ahead of God, we lose out on His plan for us in that circumstance, including experiencing His care for our hearts.
- 💙 God's blessings come with no sorrow. Debt is a big sorrow.

Questions to Consider:

1. What reservations do you have about making room for God in your finances?

2. What real or potential barriers currently exist that would prevent you from being able to tithe?

3. What is your part in overcoming those barriers?

4. Are you aware of ways the enemy is trying to steal your peace with your finances?

5. What changes might God be asking you to make in your spending habits?

6. What steps (baby steps and/or giant leaps) do you need to make to move toward financial peace?

Passages to Ponder:

"No discipline is enjoyable while it is happening—it's painful! But afterward there will be a peaceful harvest of right living for those who are trained in this way" (Hebrews 12:11).

"Good planning and hard work lead to prosperity, but hasty shortcuts lead to poverty" (Proverbs 21:5).

"The rich rules over the poor and the borrower is servant to the lender" (Proverbs 22:7).

"Better not to vow than to vow and not pay" (Ecclesiastes 5:5 NASB).

"If riches increase, do not set your heart on them" (Psalm 62:10 NIV).

"Do not wear yourself out to get rich; do not trust your own cleverness. Cast but a glance at riches, and they are gone, for they will surely sprout wings and fly off to the sky like an eagle" (Proverbs 23:4-5).

Prayer of Invitation:

Father God,

Thank You that You are my Provider. Help me to be a grateful receiver of all You have given me. Please forgive me for ways that I have robbed You in not giving back to You what is rightfully Yours. Please show me how to honor You with my finances. Change my "want to" where needed. Guide me to good solid biblical counsel and financial advice I pray. Amen.

Practice Point:

Find your version of an adult piggy bank. It could be a jar with a lid, an envelope, a special wooden box, or some other container. Purpose to give up one thing each week (a specialty coffee, a meal out, a pair of shoes …) and put that money in your piggy bank. At the end of each month, take the money out and if you're not tithing, give it to God. If you are tithing but have little to no savings, give it to yourself (not to spend but to put into savings.). Or if God prompts you, use your piggy bank as a benevolent fund to give to others.

Chapter Ten

The Surrendered Heart: Giving God Your Schedule

Few things steal rest from our hearts faster than an overcrowded schedule. Making room for God and inviting Him into your day curbs the chaos and recalibrates our hearts. Let me ask you a hypothetical question. You find yourself at home with an unexpected hour of free time (now you see why the question is hypothetical!) Do you:

> Have a nap?
> Fold laundry?
> Watch TV?
> Phone a friend?
> All of the above?

Knowing your personality type may help you answer this question and so might your gender. You've probably heard the story about the husband who says he's going to go to bed and he heads straight for the bedroom, gets undressed, and climbs into bed. His wife, on the other hand, says she's going to bed and on her way to the bedroom she stops to pick a toy that got left behind by one of their children. On the way to their bedroom to put it away, she remembers that she still needs to change the last load of laundry from the washer to the dryer. As she passes the back entry, she smells the kitty litter that is long overdue to be changed. As she grabs a bag to put the used litter into, she realizes that it is last one, so once she puts the bag in the garbage, she goes to her phone to add garbage bags to her shopping list. Only her phone won't let her access her shopping list until it completes a software update and so she…you get the picture. There is no end to tasks that need to be completed, particularly in the child-rearing years. To those of you in that stage right now, may I remind you once again that the days are long but the years are short. Regardless of what season we find ourselves in, there will always be things that require our time and attention. Busyness is not only worn as a badge of honor in our culture, it has been elevated to a hallmark of significance within our hearts. We attach our self-worth to our schedules and buy into the lie that busy is better. "One of Satan's most effective weapons in keeping us from intimacy with God and from purpose is busyness, because we don't view it as "bad." It's subtle, yet it unsuspectingly steals our focus, keeping us from stilling our hearts, which is the space God speaks into."[57]

Busy vs Rushed

In reading the gospels, it's very clear that many of Jesus' days were long and chock full of activity. He was busy indeed, but we see no evidence in Scripture that He lived a rushed life. Despite His demanding schedule, there is no account of Him hurrying or scurrying. No fussing or stewing, no harsh words said in haste, no internal churning. *Living with our heart at rest does not come as the result of the absence of activity. It's not about how much we have to do, but the attitude and stance of our heart as we are doing it.* As I write these words, pangs of conviction come to my heart as I reflect, not only on how many years I spent rushing through life, but my ongoing propensity to respond to my daily calendar with that same hasty posture of heart. I resonate deeply with the words of Kaci Nicole, "I'll pack my schedule full, then become so focused on my to-do list that I wind up living in a perpetual state of 'get to the next thing'. Other than the fact that it's an empty way to engage my schedule, this ends up presenting another problem: *my busyness creates a momentum that gets harder and harder to slow.*"[58] That internal revving that drives me to strive has regrettably, far too often, prevented me from experiencing the anchored soul, restful heart, and peaceful mind that God desired to give me. Jesus' rule of life demonstrated the only antidote that can cure the rushed revving that infects our hearts - He regularly spent time alone with the Father.

Living in the Blender

In the same way that words blur together when they are crammed on a page, so our lives can lose focus when they are blurred by a flurry of constant activity. I call that, "living in the blender." As the persistent demands on our time and energy continue to be fueled by the needs of others and our unrealistic expectations, we can begin to feel as if pieces of our heart are being cut off and swallowed up in a swirling vortex. I know the feeling only too well. In addition to the regular strains of life, the level of care our son's disability required, combined with my husband working out of town for extended periods of time, produced long seasons where my heart felt perpetually overwhelmed.

Counting the Cost

Our pace of life wreaks havoc on our hearts. While we may desire to be patient and kind, more often than not, we become impatient and even harsh as we try to maintain a frenetic pace to win an impossible game of "beat the clock." As noted earlier, if the enemy can't make us bad, he'll make us busy. And then he'll make us feel guilty for what we didn't get done or how cranky we were with those around us who felt the impact of our impatience. Don't play his games or believe his lies. Oswald Chambers observes that, "Fretting stems from our determination to have things our own way."[59] The fuller our lives and the faster we live them, the more we believe we *need* to have things go our way in order to get everything done. Such thinking reveals how inverted our hearts and minds have become from what God intended our relationship with Him to look like. Our heart's connection with God is not about getting His help to accomplish our tasks, it's about allowing God's heart and mind to permeate ours so His purposes get accomplished in and through our lives. Some people refer to this as living on mission. In very practical terms, this mindset means submitting your daily schedule to God's sovereignty and saying "God, don't bless my agenda, burn Your agenda in me." Let the story of Lazarus counsel your heart and mind. Jesus' waiting to attend to Lazarus resulted in a bigger miracle than if He had come right away and simply healed him. We miss out on so much when we force our schedule and demand our way over that of the Divine.

Depending on the quality of choices you are currently making, the items on God's agenda might look very similar to the ones on your list. Others may not. He will bring a rich clarity as you ask Him to. God is well aware of the calling and responsibilities He has placed into your life. You need not fear that He will ever ask you to shirk them. By choosing to surrender your schedule to Him, your heart will be well positioned to hear any adjustments He asks you to make.

My breath prayer (a deep longing in your soul that can be expressed in one breath) for an extended period of time was "Lord God, give me strength to do Your will." When I look back at the size of the load God gave me the grace to carry, I can confidently attest to His faithful answering of that prayer. But just as confidently, I can attest to the fact that He did not give me strength to do everything on my to-do list. My unrealistic expectations did not force His hand.

2 Corinthians 12:9 tells us that "His strength is made perfect in our weakness" and I have given Him a lot to work with! Many times, despite my best efforts and dogged determination, I still feel weak and unequal to the task He has called me to. But I've learned that if "His yoke is easy and His burden is light" (Matthew 11:28), then any weight I feel is there because I've taken it on myself, or I've let others pile it on me.

What's on Your "Stop Doing" List?

Jim Collins, renowned business leadership author and speaker, suggests that equally as important as having a focused "to-do" list is having a resolute "stop doing" list. What will you stop doing so you have room and capacity for the new items you want to add to your schedule? Where is the white space in your world? Think of your heart like a balloon, if there is enough internal pressure with no option for release, it will explode. Ask God to show you what needs to go on your "stop doing" list. Nancy Leigh DeMoss offers some insight as to what some of those items might be. Based on the verse from Song of Solomon 2:15, which says, "Catch the little foxes for us, the little foxes that spoil the vineyards ..." she encourages us to identify the *little foxes* that slyly squander our days.

"The *foxes* that steal precious time from your life may be the obvious ones—TV, movies, social media. But some may be more subtle things, like certain relationships that consume lots of time and focus but are unfruitful or worse. Or perhaps it's your children's non-stop schedules—activities intended to keep them well-rounded but that only end up burning you—and them—out. Other *foxes* that can snatch away bits and pieces of life are the toxic attitudes we allow to hang around in our hearts—the moodiness, complaining, and ingratitude that sap our energy while multiplying the time it takes to get everything done.... If you'll identify the *little foxes*, that rob you of time, margin, and spiritual vitality and if you'll purpose to eliminate those things that are unnecessarily cluttering your life—you won't have to climb over so much junk to stay flexible to God's agenda. When He calls, you'll be ready."[60]

Our lack of margin wreaks havoc on our relationships. In one of his blog posts, best-selling author and online mentor, Michael Hyatt quotes from Dr. Richard Swenson's book, *Margin: Restoring Emotional, Physical, Financial, and Time Reserves to Overloaded Lives*, Dr. Swenson describes margin like this:

> "Margin is the space between our load and our limits.
> It is the amount allowed beyond that which is needed.
> It is something held in reserve for contingencies or

unanticipated situations. Margin is the gap between rest and exhaustion, the space between breathing freely and suffocating. Margin is the opposite of overload. If we are overloaded we have no margin. Most people are not quite sure when they pass from margin to overload. Threshold points are not easily measurable and are also different for different people in different circumstances. We don't want to be under-achievers (heaven forbid!), so we fill our schedules uncritically. Options are as attractive as they are numerous, and we overbook. If we were equipped with a flashing light to indicate "100 percent full," we could better gauge our capacities. But we don't have such an indicator light, and we don't know when we have overextended until we feel the pain. As a result, many people commit to a 120 percent life and wonder why the burden feels so heavy. It is rare to see a life prescheduled to only 80 percent, leaving a margin for responding to the unexpected that God sends our way."[61]

So as someone who does not consistently allow for margin in her life, someone who packs her days so full, she's frequently checking the clock to make sure she slides in right on time, let me ask you a question I often have to ask myself, "Who would you be if you weren't 10 minutes behind life? How would margin change who you are as a person?" I think we'd be taken aback if we realized how often the person we believe ourselves to be is not the person others see. The tenderness and compassion we may feel in our hearts is often hidden by the harsh rigors of our relentless schedule. As Chuck Swindoll so fittingly discerns, "busyness rapes relationships."

I'm not suggesting that we should set our sights on multiple unscheduled hours every day, but repeatedly overbooking ourselves conveys we don't really want any of "the unexpected that God may send our way." We ask Him to help us, encourage us, and show us His favor, but when He does, we can miss it because we view it as an annoying distraction that's interrupting our chaos! In the routine of our lives, these unwanted disruptions are usually quite short but we're convinced we can't even spare a minute or two, and certainly not five or ten. Interruptions are a significant part of life, especially in the child rearing years. How do you respond to them?

Do you realize that 10 minutes is often the difference between:

A choice marked by patience vs panic. Ten minutes can be the difference between a cheerful "Good morning" and a gruff "get dressed, we're going to be late." Between "What do you want now?" and "how can I help? Between, "Seriously, another red light" and "turn up the radio, I like this song." When we're responding to our kids, it may be the difference between "What were you thinking?" and "How's your heart?" When we're standing in the long line at the grocery store, it can be the difference between showing your frustration at an incompetent clerk or extending them grace because you remember how nervous you were at your first job.

A choice marked by integrity vs indiscretion. Have you noticed how your integrity gets tested when your time gets short? The temptation to cut corners and/or push the limits increases greatly when you're pressed for time. You come to a rolling stop instead of a real stop at the STOP sign. You slide into a wheelchair parking spot convincing yourself no one will need it for the short time you'll be there. You use work time to meet a personal deadline.

A choice marked by efficiency vs emptiness. Have you been pursuing increased efficiency only to find greater emptiness? I'm all for finding more efficient ways of accomplishing the regular and often mundane tasks of our daily routines. And yes, there are times when focus and clarity in our schedules is what is needed most. However, sometimes increased efficiency is just a cloak for our desire to gain a tighter grip of control on our lives and the lives of others. In the words of Sarah Young, in *Jesus Lives*, "God's hand is the only thing you can (tightly) grasp without damaging your soul."[61] Demanding schedules destroy relationships by disengaging the level of conversation and disintegrating the rapport necessary to maintain the bond.

Our desire for enhanced productivity can also be an unconscious (and futile) attempt at achieving righteousness through accomplishment. "For by grace are ye saved, through faith and that not of yourselves. *It is a gift of God, not of works,* lest anyone should boast" (Ephesians 2:8,9 KJV) [Emphasis Mine]. Multi-tasking is admirable in moderation but any strength carried to an extreme becomes a weakness.

A choice marked by tenderness vs task. God knows we have tasks that need to get done each day. He's not trying to stop you from **all** of them; He just wants you to invite Him into your day. He wants to do life with you. He knows that a hurried heart quickly turns into harsh words. "What you say flows from what is in your heart" (Luke 6:45). When we only see the tasks ahead of us and not the people, we end up using people to accomplish our tasks and completely miss the connection our souls are craving. We also bypass opportunities to extend and receive grace, encouragement and love—all of which breathe life into our overwhelmed hearts.

Please note that all these choices are driven by margin, or lack of it, and they all impact one relationship or another. Our relationship with family members, co-workers, friends, God, and even our own souls are all affected. Many of the stresses in our day are self-induced by our own lack of margin, and often times only about 10 minutes is the difference. So, I ask you, "Is all that chaos really worth hitting the snooze button?" Of course, it's about more than hitting the snooze button, but that's a practical tip which can really address the morning chaos that often fills our homes.

Underlying all those choices is an attitude of our heart that allows us to find rest in knowing God can be trusted with all things, even with our schedule. Psalm 39:5-7 offers an apt perspective, "My life is no longer than the width of my hand. An entire lifetime is just a moment to you; human existence is but a breath. We are merely moving shadows, and all our busy rushing ends in nothing. We heap up wealth for someone else to spend. And so, Lord, where do I put my hope? My only hope is in You."

Margin does not come easy. You will have to revisit your "stop doing list" often, identifying and addressing the little foxes in your life. And, just because you have some time open up in your schedule doesn't mean you need to fill it with something else. God may be creating time to just be with you. Don't fear the white space. We like to spend time with people we love, people who know us and make us feel special for who we are. God wants you to know He's one of those people. He loves you, He knows you and He delights in you. (Zephaniah 3:17)

Stepping out of the Blender

How do I step out of the blender? How do I stop the revving inside me? I know there has got to be a better way to live, but it seems out of reach, how do I get there? These are questions you may be asking and these are the questions I have asked myself countless times. The answers are both much more simple and much more difficult than I expected. After expressing my frustrated and overwhelmed heart to my mentor, she challenged me to spend 10 minutes three times a week in solitude and silence. She suggested I find a comfortable chair, preferably in front of a window where I could feel the sun on my face. She recommended I sit with my palms face up on my lap as an outward sign of my heart's desire to receive from the Lord. This was to be time where I sat quietly before the Lord. Prayers for myself and others could take place at another time, but this was to be time reserved for Him and His agenda. Seemed like a simple enough request, so I gave it a try. I had no idea how long 10 minutes could be when your mind is racing and your heart is restless. I wrestled with thoughts like, *this is crazy, do you know how much work I could be getting done if I wasn't just sitting here!* and *I don't think I'm wired for this.* But I persevered, not wanting to have to tell my mentor I didn't do what she had asked me to. It was clumsy and awkward at first but I cannot tell you the depth to which this simple exercise has transformed my life. It's not that some magical, mystical experience happened just because I sat down. It was a simple act of obedience that made room for God to pour into my life what was so desperately lacking. I just needed to position myself to receive all that He had for me.

How Do We Position Ourselves to Receive from God? God desperately wants to pour His power and Spirit into us to mold us into the person He designed us to be. It's His job to provide the transforming power and the encouragement of His Spirit. It's our job to position ourselves to receive from Him.

Be still and know that I am God (Psalm 46:10). We know that verse well but we often live like it's a suggestion rather than God's wise command to us. Imagine trying to fill a watering can with your garden hose just as the wind comes up and blows it across the yard. It's hard to fill a moving bucket! Only God can slow the revving inside of us but there's something about being physically still and quiet that makes it easier for our heart to follow suit.

Saturate your soul with God's Word. I cannot emphasize strongly enough the importance of reading and memorizing Scripture. How can you know God's heart for you if you don't read His love letter to you? You will not want to change the way you spend or give your time until you gain a sense of God's goodness and His love floods your soul. Re-wallpapering your mind with the truths of God's Word brings the perspective your soul needs to trust when you can't see the way ahead. Do you know Jesus as the Lover of your soul and the Lifter of your head? (Psalm 3:3) Spending time in His Word and in His presence allows those to be more than just words on a page. "I wait for the Lord, my soul waits and in His word I put my hope. My soul waits for the Lord more than watchmen wait for the morning" (Psalm 130:5-6).

Come to God with an attitude of expectancy. In chapter five, we learned that to be expectant is an expression of faith, anchored in our trust in God's goodness and His power, His character, and His desire for our lives. *I'm convinced if we could actually grasp all God desires for us, combined with His power to bring those desires to pass, we would come running with bold humility to sit before Him.* "In the morning, LORD, You hear my voice; in the morning I lay my requests before You and wait expectantly" (Psalm 5:3).

ACTRESS

You may be familiar with the prayer acronym ACTS—adoration, confession, thanksgiving, and supplication. I have found this tool helpful in keeping my prayer times more focused as well as being effective at reminding me of what to pray that I might not otherwise think to pray about. In recent years, I have tweaked the acronym to include a few additional elements that reflect the journey of my heart. I offer it to you in hopes that it will serve as a helpful framework as you spend time with the Father.

A—Adoration. I spend some time praising God for all He is and how that impacts my life. "What mighty praise, O God, belongs to You in Zion" (Psalm 65:1). I praise Him as my Redeemer, Deliverer, the Source of all wisdom, and power or that He knows what my heart needs most from Him. I praise Him for His faithfulness or His protection or His provision or whatever comes to my heart and mind in the moment. This brief time of worship serves as a catalyst for the shift in the posture of my heart that is necessary for me to come into His presence. God "inhabits the praises of His people" (Psalm 22:3 KJV). If that's where He lives, that's where I come to meet Him.

C—Confession. If I'm not already aware of what I need to confess, I ask Him to show me the sins lurking in my heart (Psalm 19:12). This request is definitely not an exercise in self-deprecation or false guilt but rather an intentional choice to keep short accounts with God. I don't want anything to block the flow of God's full hand of blessing in my life (because I know how desperately I need it!) and sin does that. Psalm 66:18 reminds us that, "If I had not confessed the sin in my heart, my Lord would not have listened" (NLT). Praying with known, unconfessed sin in our hearts is like trying to have a phone conversation with someone while your mute button is on.

T—Thanksgiving. I specifically thank God for what He's done in my day to day life. "I will thank You, Lord, with all my heart; I will tell of all the marvelous things you have done" (Psalm 9:1 NLT). I thank Him for how the sunshine makes my heart come alive after several cloudy, gray days or for a great conversation with my husband or a friend or how He brought just the right words or verses of Scripture to mind when I needed them or an unexpected opportunity that He brought my way that He knew would encourage me or .... Thanksgiving helps me better focus on His care for me and the attentiveness with which He provides that care. It cultivates an attitude of gratitude that changes both the outlook of my heart and its inward focus.

R—Resist the Enemy. James 4:7 tells us to "humble ourselves before God. Resist the devil and he will flee from you." We do not need to live in fear of the enemy of our souls because "greater is He that is in us, than He that is in the world" (1 John 4:4 KJV) but to ignore his schemes is to leave our hearts and lives precariously exposed. I remind the Devil often that because of the covering of the shed blood of Christ, he has no power or authority in our home, our marriage, our finances or our future. I line up behind the cross and lean into the truth of God's Word that tells us, "no weapon formed against us shall prosper" (Isaiah 54:17 KJV); our "weapons are not carnal, but mighty in God for pulling down strongholds" (1 Corinthians 10:4 NIV); that God "disarmed the spiritual rulers and authorities. He shamed them publicly by His victory over them on the cross" (Colossians 2:15). As I remind the enemy of these truths, my mind is reminded too. That helps me guard my heart from the lies he tries to throw at me.

E—Envision your day and invite God into it. "Many are the plans in a person's heart, but it is the LORD's purpose that prevails" (Proverbs 19:21 NIV). As I look into the day ahead of me, I invite God into each part of it—the meetings, the appointments, the conversations, the things I'm looking forward to, and those I dread. I thank Him that He promises to walk with me through them all, and I surrender my schedule to His sovereignty. "Lord, don't bless my agenda; burn Your agenda in me."

S—Supplication. Supplication is a word used in the King James Version of Philippians 4:6, which means request or petition. "But in everything by prayer and supplication, with thanksgiving, let your requests be made known to God." This is God's invitation for us to bring to Him the people and circumstances that are on our heart. This is where I pray for my family, my friends, my future, and my fears. Through the years, this process has reshaped the tone of my prayers and now talking with God feels more like a conversation and less like a shopping list.

S—Sit with your Savior. Now that you've had your turn to talk, you need to allow God time to speak into your heart. This is a time when you are quiet before Him, giving Him opportunity to pour into you what He is longing to give you and what you so desperately need. I urge you, do not seek an experience, seek God. Come out of obedience and an understanding of your need. Let Him set the agenda for your time together. Sometimes it might be vibrant and other times, quite nondescript.

Like me, you may think you have no time for sitting. I confess I still fight the resistance in my heart and the items on my to-do list. It's amazing how many other things I can find to do when I could be sitting with my Savior. Ten minutes is not the magic number. Our lives flex and change on a regular basis and there are seasons that allow more time than others. It's not about the legalism of the time, it's about *regularly* giving God room in our schedule. Treating our time as our gift to God and others changes the way we use it. Understanding the value of solitude, reflection, and listening prayer no longer make them luxuries on our calendar. They are essential to guarding our heart. It's like sitting in the sun. We don't realize its impact, but others can see it on our face.

Practical Tips:
- Develop a "stop doing list."
- Decide in advance when the best time of day is for you to sit with your Savior. Set realistic goals and grant yourself grace.
- Identify the *foxes* that are stealing your time.
- Set your alarm 10 minutes earlier (and don't hit the snooze button)
- Develop a Tech Time Budget. Decide in advance how many hours you will spend in front of technology for the

purpose of entertainment each day (TV, Computer, phone) and stick to it. Invite someone to hold you accountable.

- Determine areas where you need to increase efficiency in your life and ask for help in doing it.

Key Learnings:

❤ Just because we have some time open up in our schedule doesn't mean we need to fill it.

❤ Don't ask God to bless your agenda, ask Him to burn His agenda in you.

❤ It's hard to fill a moving bucket.

❤ Solitude, reflection, and listening prayer are not luxuries on our calendars. They are essential to guarding our hearts.

❤ Treating our time as our gift to God and others changes the way we use it. We are more inclined to invest it rather than spend it.

Questions to Consider:

1. Who would you be if you weren't 10 minutes behind life? Unpack that idea in your mind.

2. What's on your "stop doing" list?

3. What areas in your life require more efficiency? Who can help you with that?

4. How might incorporating ACTRESS into your life help stop the revving in your heart?

5. What steps do you need to take to make room in your schedule to sit with your Savior?

Passages to Ponder

"For everything there is a season, a time for every activity under heaven. A time to be born and a time to die. A time to plant and a time to harvest. A time to kill and a time to heal. A time to tear down and a time to build up. A time to cry and a time to laugh. A time to grieve and a time to dance. A time to scatter stones and a time to gather stones. A time to embrace and a time to turn away. A time to search and a time to quit searching. A time to keep and a time to throw away. A time to tear and a time to mend. A time to be quiet and a time to speak. A time to love and a time to hate. A time for war and a time for peace. What do people really get for all their hard work? I have seen the burden God has placed on us all" (Eccl. 3:1-10).

"I wait for the Lord, my whole being waits, and in His word I put my hope. I wait for the Lord more than watchmen wait for the morning, more than watchmen wait for the morning" (Psalm 130:5-6).

Prayer of Invitation:

Lord Jesus,
You know how much I long to "step out of the blender." Thank You that You made it possible. Help me to believe that it's possible for me. Please show me the steps You want me to take to build solitude, reflection, and listening prayer into my schedule. Please forgive me for constantly asking You to bless my agenda. O God, please burn Your agenda in me. Guide me, I pray, as I learn to "Sit with my Savior." Amen.

Practice Point:

I extend to you the same challenge that was presented to me. Three times a week, spend 10 minutes sitting with your Savior. Come before Him, laying your expectations and agenda aside. Place your hands, palms face up on your lap, to reflect a posture of willingness to receive. This is a time when you are quiet before Him, giving Him opportunity to pour into you what He is longing to give you and what you so desperately need. I remind you once again, do not seek an experience; seek God.

Chapter Eleven

The Supported Heart: Embracing Spiritual Friendship

God's heart for us has always included the encouragement and support of others in our lives. His design, as modeled in the Trinity, has been one of mutual support. He knew our hearts would need the prayer, input, and accountability that other godly people can bring into our lives. He also knew pouring into others' lives would bring the growth and fulfillment our hearts need to feel fully alive.

Many of the principles we have discussed so far are counter cultural and you may be wondering if you have the strength to swim upstream. If that describes how you're feeling, take encouragement from God's provision in the life of Moses. Exodus chapter 17 records the account of the Israelites being attacked by their enemies, the Amalekites. Moses, who was now getting on in years, gives Joshua the command to rally the troops and go out and fight. He then tells him that he (Moses) and his brother Aaron, along with their comrade Hur, will be on the top of a nearby hill with his staff pointed heavenward. The staff was a symbol of power and was used in many of the miracles God performed through Moses. We read in verse 11 that, "As long as Moses held up the staff with his hands, the Israelites had the advantage. But whenever he lowered his hands, the Amalekites gained the upper hand." As you can imagine, the longer the battle raged on, despite Moses' best intentions, his arms became weary. Notice what Aaron and Hur did next. They "found a stone for him to sit on. Then they stood on each side, *holding up his hands* until sunset." (vs. 12). [Emphasis Mine]. As a result, Joshua and his troops were able to soundly defeat their enemy.

There will be days and seasons in each of our lives that, despite our best efforts and intentions to live God's way and keep our focus on Him, we will become weary, overwhelmed, and discouraged. It is then that we need an Aaron or a Hur. Someone to lift up our weary arms. Someone to encourage us and remind us of the character and power of the God we serve. Someone to help us recognize the work of the enemy and point us heavenward to access the authority we need to defeat his plans for our demise. We need a spiritual friend.

What is Spiritual Friendship?

Despite its countless nuances, we all have a general understanding of what typical friendship is. What uniquely defines spiritual friendship is the aspect of *doing life together on a heart level.* A spiritual friend is a person who not only cares about the happenings of your life, but also cares about the impact those experiences have on your spiritual heart. A spiritual friend is a person who cares deeply about you and demonstrates that your heart matters to them by the way they engage, encourage, and exhort you. You may be asking, *do such people really exist?* The answer is yes and indeed, they are a precious find. Richard Foster describes their rarity in his book, *Celebration of Discipline.* He notes that "Superficiality is the curse of our age …. The desperate need today is not for a greater number of intelligent people, or gifted people, but for deep people."[62] The depth he's referring to here is a depth of character and a depth of relationship with Christ. While spiritual friends are neither perfect nor plenteous, they are also not shallow and they are able to look beyond themselves. Your happiness matters to them but not more than your holiness.

David and Jonathan

Spiritual friendship is not a fad or a new concept. It dates back to David and Jonathan. Their story is recorded in 1 Samuel 20 and recounts the time when David was fleeing Jonathan's father, Saul, who was trying to kill David because David had been anointed to be the next king. The story reads like a novel and models the depths and deeds of spiritual friendship. As you read it, take special note of how David and Jonathan's spiritual friendship influenced their thoughts and actions:

David now fled from Naioth in Ramah and found Jonathan. "What have I done?" he exclaimed. "What is my crime? How have I offended your father that he is so determined to kill me?"

"That's not true!" Jonathan protested. "You're not going to die. He always tells me everything he's going to do, even the little things. I know my father wouldn't hide something like this from me. It just isn't so!" Then David took an oath before Jonathan and said, "Your father knows perfectly well about our friendship, so he has said to himself, 'I won't tell Jonathan—why should I hurt him?' But I swear to you that I am only a step away from death! I swear it by the Lord and by your own soul!"

"Tell me what I can do to help you," Jonathan exclaimed.

David replied, "Tomorrow we celebrate the new moon festival. I've always eaten with the king on this occasion, but tomorrow I'll hide in the field and stay there until the evening of the third day. If your father asks where I am, tell him I asked permission to go home to Bethlehem for an annual family sacrifice. If he says, 'Fine!' you will know all is well. But if he is angry and loses his temper, you will know he is determined to kill me. Show me this loyalty as my sworn friend—for we made a solemn pact before the Lord—or kill me yourself if I have sinned against your father. But please don't betray me to him!"

"Never!" Jonathan exclaimed. "You know that if I had the slightest notion my father was planning to kill you, I would tell you at once."

Then David asked, "How will I know whether or not your father is angry?"

"Come out to the field with me," Jonathan replied. And they went out there together. Then Jonathan told David, "I promise by the LORD, the God of Israel, that by this time tomorrow, or the next day at the latest, I will talk to my father and let you know at once how he feels about you. If he speaks favorably about you, I will let you know. But if he is angry and wants you killed, may the LORD strike me and even kill me if I don't warn you so you can escape and live. May the LORD be with you as he used to be with my father. And may you treat me with the faithful love of the LORD as long as I live. But if I die, treat my family with this faithful love, even when the LORD destroys all your enemies from the face of the earth."

So Jonathan made a solemn pact with David, saying, "May the LORD destroy all your enemies!" And Jonathan made David reaffirm his vow of friendship again, for Jonathan loved David as he loved himself.

Then Jonathan said, "Tomorrow we celebrate the new moon festival. You will be missed when your place at the table is empty. The day after tomorrow, toward evening, go to the place where you hid before, and wait there by the stone pile. I will come out and shoot three arrows to the side of the stone pile as though I were shooting at a target. Then I will send a boy to bring the arrows back. If you hear me tell him, 'They're on this side,' then you will know, as surely as the LORD lives, that all is well, and there is no trouble. But if I tell him, 'Go farther—the arrows are still ahead of you,' then it will mean that you must leave immediately, for the LORD is sending you away. And may the LORD make us keep our promises to each other, for he has witnessed them."

So David hid himself in the field, and when the new moon festival began, the king sat down to eat. He sat at his usual place against the wall, with Jonathan sitting opposite him and Abner beside him. But David's place was empty. Saul didn't say anything about it that day, for he said to himself, "Something must have made David ceremonially unclean." But when David's place was empty again the next day, Saul asked Jonathan, "Why hasn't the son of Jesse been here for the meal either yesterday or today?"

Jonathan replied, "David earnestly asked me if he could go to Bethlehem. He said, 'Please let me go, for we are having a family sacrifice. My brother demanded that I be there. So please let me get away to see my brothers.' That's why he isn't here at the king's table."

Saul boiled with rage at Jonathan. "You stupid son of a whore!" he swore at him. "Do you think I don't know that you want him to be king in your place, shaming yourself and your mother? As long as that son of Jesse is alive, you'll never be king. Now go and get him so I can kill him!"

"But why should he be put to death?" Jonathan asked his father. "What has he done?" Then Saul hurled his spear at Jonathan, intending to kill him. So at last Jonathan realized that his father was really determined to kill David.

Jonathan left the table in fierce anger and refused to eat on that second day of the festival, for he was crushed by his father's shameful behavior toward David.

The next morning, as agreed, Jonathan went out into the field and took a young boy with him to gather his arrows. "Start running," he told the boy, "so you can find the arrows as I shoot them." So the boy ran, and Jonathan shot an arrow beyond him. When the boy had almost reached the arrow, Jonathan shouted, "The arrow is still ahead of you. Hurry, hurry, don't wait." So the boy quickly gathered up the arrows and ran back to his master. He, of course, suspected nothing; only Jonathan and David understood the signal. Then Jonathan gave his bow and arrows to the boy and told him to take them back to town.

As soon as the boy was gone, David came out from where he had been hiding near the stone pile. Then David bowed three times to Jonathan with his face to the ground. Both of them were in tears as they embraced each other and said good-bye, especially David.

At last Jonathan said to David, "Go in peace, for we have sworn loyalty to each other in the LORD's name. The LORD is the witness of a bond between us and our children forever." Then David left, and Jonathan returned to the town.

The Impact of Spiritual Friendship

While there are many principles that we could procure from this passage, I would like to highlight just a few key outcomes of genuine spiritual friendship and how they personally impacted David and Jonathan. Of particular note is what distinguishes their friendship, moving it beyond what we might consider just another close relationship. Notice how the Lord was included in their oaths, their conversations, and their plans. He was the source of the depth of their bond.

Note also that their spiritual friendship:

1) brought comfort and courage to David. I cannot imagine how agonizing it was for David to sit out there in the field waiting by the stone pile, his mind waging war with *what ifs*. The risk of betrayal was very real and its implications were life threatening. Yet knowing his heart *really* mattered to Jonathan brought him comfort and courage, allowing him to stay the course. Spiritual friendships help us stay the course when life has a way of throwing us off kilter. Just as David knew he could rely on Jonathan and his promise, because it was an oath before the Lord, the reliability of our spiritual friends supports us when God asks us to take courageous steps in our faith journey.

2) brought perspective and peace to Jonathan. At first, Jonathan was quick to dismiss David's accusations but the depth of their friendship prompted him to investigate the matter further. He did not let the adage "blood is thicker than water" cloud his search for truth. Once he discovered what was really going on, he was able to see the danger from David's perspective and move forward with the spiritual insight and strength of character afforded by his commitment to honoring the Lord.

For Jonathan, doing the right thing required a lot of potentially life-altering choices. By sparing David's life, Jonathan was giving up the throne for himself. When he called down curses on David's enemies, he was doing so on his own father. In that culture when a new king was crowned, all his enemies, *and their families* were killed. Jonathan made David reconfirm his covenant with him because otherwise Jonathan and his family would be killed when David became king. The risk of betrayal was real for Jonathan, too, but he had peace that David would honor his covenant with him. Truly, theirs was a precious bond. Their choices not only changed the trajectory of their lives, but their children's lives as well. While the stakes are not likely to be quite as high in our spiritual friendships, doing life with spiritual friends *will* impact the big decisions of our life. It has the potential to change the direction of our lives and the lives of our children.

You may be asking, "Where do I find a spiritual friend?" Before you start your search, let's consider some of the road blocks or barriers that hinder meaningful spiritual friendships.

Barriers to Spiritual Friendship

> **B**elieving the enemy's lies
> **A**llowing your attitude to get in the way
> **R**eliving the past
> **R**esisting God's promptings
> **I**ndifference to God's design for community
> **E**xpecting the wrong thing
> **R**efusing to receive from God and others
> **S**elf-made plans

Believing the Enemy's Lies

No one would want to be my spiritual friend if they really knew me. This statement is classic enemy deception. We see everyone else's seemingly pristine life through the peep hole they allow us to see through and when we compare that to knowing the whole messy state of our lives, we consistently come up lacking. Remind yourself, that they only see the shiny side of your life and they are probably looking at you the same way you are looking at them. That's the gift of spiritual friendship. As it grows, you learn more about each other, warts, wrinkles, foibles, and all, which makes you feel more connected to each other. As you share struggles and the lessons God has taught you through them, you become even more endeared to one another. As you look to God's Word together and pray for each other, your hearts are touched, your spirits are encouraged and your faith is strengthened.

There's nobody out there for me. Don't assume you know something God doesn't or that His power is limited to your perspective. Consider the role fear or resistance may be playing in your thought processes. The only thing that limits God's gift to you is your willingness to receive it.

This won't work. How can you be so sure? I have yet to meet a person engaged in a meaningful spiritual friendship who has not found it to be both life giving and incredibly significant in their life. Ponder the possibility of unrealistic expectations influencing your point of view.

I am invisible. I have felt that way, too. The enemy would like us to believe that God doesn't see us either. Resist that lie with the truth of God's Word. Psalm 139 tells us "O Lord, You have examined my heart and know everything about me…You know my every thought…How precious are Your thoughts *about me* Oh God" (vs 1,2,17).

I don't know what to do. While spiritual friendship is not a new idea, it is a foreign concept to many of us. Keep reading and ask God for wisdom. I believe He will bring the clarity you are looking for. Don't complicate things. Be yourself and be a friend.

This is just for weak people. I thought so, too, until God allowed the circumstances of my life to open my eyes so I could understand my strong, self-sufficient, and maverick approach to life was in direct opposition to His best for me. I still consider myself to be a strong woman but my spiritual friends have helped me to be a strong woman who receives counsel, accountability, and encouragement. Their input in my life adds depth and breadth to my strength.

My situation is different. You may feel your circumstances are so unique, it would be impossible for anyone to understand your heart. I can relate. As the mother of two special needs children and a husband who used to work out of town most of the time, I was convinced that no one would be able to really *get* me. But God knows you, *gets* you and knows what you need most. He is Jehovah Roi—the God who sees. "The Lord keeps watch over you as you come and go, both now and forever "(Psalm 121:8).

My heart doesn't matter. Your heart may have been battered by life to the point you no longer believe there is any value in it. If that is the case, may I just say, "I'm sorry for the depth of your pain." Please read and reread Psalm 139 in its entirety until its truth soaks into your soul. Review some of the teaching from chapter one and purpose to "Above all else guard your heart for it is the well spring of life" (Proverbs 4:23).

It takes too much work. Yes, it will be work but like Moses, the work of developing those friendships will be worth it. Aaron and Hur were there when he needed them most. Ecclesiastes 4:10 reminds us that "If one falls down, his friend can help him up. But pity the man who falls and has no one to help him up!" When the unexpected happens in your life, who is on your call list? Who will be there to walk with you on the unforeseen legs of your life journey?

If I open up emotionally, I'm scared I'll drown in the intensity. If you don't open up, you might explode internally and that would be even messier! Becoming spiritual friends with someone does not require that you instantly share the depth of your heart. As the warmth of your friendship grows, you can navigate the level of openness in a way that is mutually satisfying. Tears shared among spiritual friends are part of what strengthens your bond.

I'm not spiritual enough for this. In our own strength, this would be true. It's Christ living inside of us, and His Spirit working within us that gives us anything of value to share with others. Your life experiences and your ability to testify to God's goodness and power is more significant than you think. They are what qualify you as a spiritual friend. One of the many benefits of spiritual friendship is it causes you to grow in your walk with Christ. Part of what creates the connection between you is learning together.

Allowing your Attitude to Get in the Way

What's your mentality on neediness? I shared earlier that I lived much of my early adult life believing I didn't really need other people. I had extremely high standards for myself and heaven forbid I should ever be perceived as needy! When I got married, things improved slightly but my husband can attest to the fact that my independence did not evaporate at the altar. God has had much to teach me in this area. I have learned that our longing for connection—to be heard and understood—is not a selfish, unrealistic expectation. Rather, it is a God-given emotional **need** that has been placed in each of us, especially women. Reflect again on the emotional needs of the personality overview in chapter seven and you will see that although each style is unique, connection with others is vital for all of them.

I don't have time for this. One of the enemy's greatest tactics/weapons in our life is isolation and nothing is more isolating than a relentless schedule. Just like a wolf knows a sheep will be more vulnerable if it can separate it from the herd, the enemy knows how susceptible we become to his plans when we think no one is watching. Beyond that, a spiritual friend can help you recognize the enemy's schemes when you can't see them.

What if they say no? While this question is a real question, it is one borne out of fear and/or pride. We'll talk more about this a little later but understand that if someone says no, it's not a reflection on you. God has other plans and He is helping to bring clarity by narrowing the choices. Remember their "no" may be an indication they are not in a place to give your heart the care and attention it requires. By them saying no, you're saving yourself the pain of even greater disappointment and a difficult conversation later.

Reliving the Past

Letting tradition hold us back. As I mentioned earlier, spiritual friendship is not a new strategy or the latest relationship cure. Still, there can be a lingering sense in our hearts of *I've never done anything like this before.* I felt the same way. I don't have a sister and the idea of connecting with other women on that level just felt a little too soft for me. I grew up in a farming community with a lot of my family living within an hour of my home. By virtue of geography, our lives used to be focused a lot more on community than they are now. Since moving away, I've needed to become more intentional in pursuing the community those relationships brought to my life.

I've been hurt before. If you've had your trust broken or felt the sting of betrayal, I can hear your heart screaming, *I'm not doing that again.* You do need to be wise in what you share with whom and when, but that does not mean that you can/should stay isolated. Doing so plays right into the enemy's hand and forfeits the opportunity for healing and restoration. As a reminder to all of us, Proverbs 18:8 teaches that, "The words of a gossip are like choice morsels; they go down to a man's inmost parts." In other words, they cut to the core. In order for us to be a good spiritual friend, we need to be trustworthy ourselves, always mindful of the Golden Rule, "Do unto others as you would have them do unto you."

Resisting God's Promptings

Sometimes we ask God for His help but then don't do what He asks. We don't respond to the promptings He gives us and then we get upset with Him for His apparent lack of concern. James 1:5 tells us that if we lack wisdom, we simply need to ask for it and He will give it to us without criticizing us or reprimanding us for asking. So, if we're honest, the issue is either we are not asking for God's wisdom or we are not following through on the direction He has already provided. How many times have you sensed a restlessness, a Holy discontent in your heart and you've ignored it because you didn't understand it, so you didn't pursue it? What about the times, you thought to yourself, *I should call* _____ *or get to know them better*, but you dismissed the idea until a more convenient time? Perhaps it was a compliment or word of encouragement that God prompted you to share but you passed over the opportunity because you were too rushed. Maybe He was prompting you to not say something, like those harsh, stinging words that just flashed into your mind, but you barreled right through and let them have it. Then you disregarded His urging to ask for forgiveness. When we resist God's promptings, we close the door on God's best for our relationship with Him and with others.

Indifference to God's design for community

What you're really saying is, "All that sounds OK for others but I can do this on my own; I don't need a spiritual friend." The model of the Trinity begs the question that if God designed community to be something that He lives in all the time, why wouldn't we need others in our lives too? Seclusion diminishes who God made us to be. Beyond the need to avoid isolation, consider who you have in your life to keep you accountable to God's Word and His ways?' Knowing that the "spirit is willing, but the body is weak" (Matthew 26:41), it is spiritually naïve to think we can consistently navigate the landmines of life and the enemy's schemes without someone pointing us back to Christ when we waver. Proverbs 18:24 advises us that, "A man of many companions may come to ruin, but there is a friend who sticks closer than a brother." *Companions don't always ask the hard questions: spiritual friends who care about your heart do!*

Expecting the Wrong Thing

Not your new best friend. A spiritual friend is not necessarily a new best friend that you phone regularly or take shopping. While you may spend some social time together, the focus of your relationship is building a spiritual bond.

A spiritual friend will not have the answers to all of your problems. Please do not plug your spiritual umbilical cord into your spiritual friend. The nourishment your soul needs comes from God alone. A spiritual friend is there to encourage you and point you to Jesus, not to serve as His stand in. The quickest way to destroy a spiritual friendship is to put undue pressure on someone to meet the needs only God can supply.

Spiritual friendship is not a mentor/mentee relationship. The learning and encouragement goes both ways. It is mutual. It's not about finding someone you think will be able to build deeply into you without you investing in their life, too. You both bring your lives and your love for Jesus to the table and enjoy a shared meal. This is not a restaurant experience where one pays the other for their service.

Your problems won't go away. Just because you're engaged in spiritual friendship and are enjoying the blessings that come with such sweet fellowship, your problems will not disappear. Bearing one another's burdens only makes sense if there are burdens to carry. However, spiritual friends can help us uncover our blind spots so we can see issues in our lives that are self-induced.

The relationship will not blossom overnight. If you are entering into a spiritual friendship with someone you don't know well, give it time to germinate and take root. If you enter into a spiritual friendship with someone you do know well, also give it time to germinate and take root. Neither situation will be an instant pudding solution. It's one thing to talk about the weather and the routine happenings of life; it's quite another thing to talk about the deep issues of our heart. Trust is built over time; don't rush it. Rushing the process is like trying to peel a peach that hasn't ripened yet. It's very difficult and what's inside is not as sweet as we'd hoped.

Struggle will be part of your shared journey. You will make mistakes, and so will they. You may both have godly intentions, but you are also both flawed human beings whose propensity to sin will remain alive and well until the day God calls you home. Forgiveness and difficult conversations are the soil in which the depth of your relationship grows.

Refusing to Receive from God and Others.

How do you receive correction? Do you have a teachable spirit? Are you a Justifier, a Deflector, or a Stuffer? Any and all of these responses will limit your ability to receive what God and others desire to pour into your life. The value of a spiritual friend is not always that they teach you something new, but rather they remind you of things that you already know but may have forgotten amidst the struggle. They may even give you what Larry Crabb calls the last 10%. That's the hard truth which often gets left unsaid. Giving the last 10% is not license to be harsh and unkind but rather comes from a heart of love whose deep desire is to seek God's truth about the situation and help their spiritual friend choose God's best for them. "Perfume and incense bring joy to the heart, and the pleasantness of one's friend springs from his earnest counsel" (Proverbs 27:9). "Wounds from a friend can be trusted, but an enemy multiplies kisses" (Proverbs 27:6).

How do you receive a compliment or help from others? Receiving kind words or practical assistance from others may not be easy. Do we accept it, explain it away, or outright refuse it? (Ladies, be honest, how many of you would be completely comfortable receiving housekeeping help from a friend knowing they'd be cleaning your bathroom and other private areas of your home?)

The Apostle Paul, whom we learned had a very independent and high achieving choleric personality, had his independence stripped away from him multiple times when he was being transported as a prisoner. With his freedom taken away, he now had to depend on others to provide his care. "He ordered an officer to keep Paul in custody but to give him some freedom and allow his friends to visit him and take care of his needs" (Acts 24:23). "The next day when we docked at Sidon, Julius was very kind to Paul and let him go ashore to visit with friends so they could provide for his needs" (Acts 27:3). Our ability to receive either correction or encouragement is a direct reflection of the posture of our hearts—whether it's turned in submission toward God or bent in independence away from Him.

Self-made Plans

Spiritual Friendship is not a program. It is a relationship as unique as the people who are involved in it. How you engage will not always look the same. While the principles of spiritual friendship may be replicated, the specifics most certainly cannot be. Some may choose to do a Bible study together, others may meet for regular prayer times. Some may develop a few meaningful questions that guide their discussion, such as, "What has happened in your life since we last met?" or "How is your heart?" or "What is God teaching you?" and "How can I pray for you?" It may look like some of these things or it might look entirely different. The critical element is that you commit to meeting regularly to learn about and care for each other's heart.

Don't expect God to work on your timeline. This is another time you need to pray and ask the Lord to bring your timeline into alignment with His. I remember feeling very impatient in my search for a spiritual friend. I was lonely and feeling overwhelmed so I kept looking at different women in our church thinking, *Is that her? Should I talk to her? Maybe, it's her.* Looking back, I see the angst I caused for myself by trying to help God. My counsel would be to let things bubble up so that the relationship grows out of the overflow of what God is stirring in you and others rather than the connection being contrived. None of us gets to decide how, when and with whom God works, but we can know it will be good if He's in the center of it. If you always have to be in control, then all you can have is what you can manufacture and that leaves no room for what God can do.

PIE in the Sky?

Let's look at some concrete steps to help move the concept of spiritual friendship beyond a pie-in-the-sky idea. You cannot put flesh and skin on something if there are no bones underneath to provide support. The foundation of spiritual friendship is the same as it is for any other significant spiritual initiative in our lives— prayer. James 5:16 teaches us that "The prayer of a righteous man is powerful and effective." Please do not dismiss prayer as a nice extra for when you have time, for *much* happens when we pray. "Prayer is abandoning my reliance on me and running toward the rest that can be found only when I rely on the power of God."[63]

Pray, Pray, Pray

... for direction. Ask God to prepare your heart and the heart of the person He intends to be your spiritual friend. Ask Him for courage (remembering that you can't be brave until you're scared first). Ask Him for a clear understanding of what your heart needs and the qualities you would be looking for in a spiritual friend. As you talk with God about this, it deepens your relationship with Him and increases your sense of His care for your heart. James reminds us that "we have not because we ask not" (James 4:2-3 KJV).

... for specific connections. The person God would have you connect with in spiritual friendship might be someone you haven't met yet or it might be someone right under your nose. Strategizing to figure out who that person is or the right timing to ask them without praying will only cause anxiety and disillusionment to rise up within you. Remind yourself again, "Oh, how great are God's riches and wisdom and knowledge! How impossible it is for us to understand his decisions and his ways!" (Romans 11:33). Relationships such as these happen "Not by might, nor by power, but by my spirit, saith the LORD of hosts" (Zechariah 4:6 KJV). Invite God's Spirit to guide you in this process and make His way clear to you.

... against the enemy. The enemy knows the impact of a person whose heart is committed to Christ and supported by fellow believers. As such, he will do whatever he can to thwart our desire for deep and meaningful spiritual friendship. We need not live in fear of that because God's Word tells us that "greater is He that is in us, than he that is in the world" (1 John 4:4). We need to be mindful of it, put on our spiritual armor (Ephesians 6), and stand firm. Thank the Lord that He has defeated Satan, that His plans will prevail, and that "no weapon formed against us shall prosper" (Isaiah 54:17).

Identify your specific barriers.

Review the list of barriers provided above and ask the Lord to show you which one(s) are hindering you from engaging in spiritual friendship. He may even show you barriers that are different than the ones identified here. Whatever they are, be intentional about confessing and addressing them. If you don't, not only will you lose out, but someone else will lose out on the gift of you. When we admit to ourselves and to others the barriers that persistently trip us up, exposing them seems to loosen their grip. "Therefore confess your sins to each other and pray for each other so that you may be healed" (James 5:16A).

Envision the culture you desire. When I'm teaching this material at a ladies retreat, it's at this point that I engage in some Q&A with them, discussing how they would like spiritual friendship to impact the culture of their church. I start by reminding them, as I do you, "Where there is no vision, the people perish" (Proverbs 29:18). At first, they struggle to wrap their minds around the potential spiritual friendship has to change their current environment, but one by one, as they start throwing out ideas, momentum starts to build. That is also the time when some of them realize what barriers they have erected and how those barriers have negatively influenced others. Often they will get up and go spend some time in the prayer room. I always request that there be a designated prayer room at each retreat, and I let them know at the beginning of the weekend that it is more important they hear what God has to say to them than listening to me. I say that to you as well. If there is some business you need to do with God, please respond to His conviction on your heart. Put down the book and spend some time dealing with the issues He's brought to your attention. Confession and repentance bring clarity, renew hope, and restore vision.

Consider how your life may be different if you had someone who cared deeply about your spiritual growth. Reflect on what it would be like to care deeply about someone else's walk with God. Mull over in your mind what your expectations would be for that kind of connection in your life. If you do not have a sense of vision around spiritual friendship, sit with your Savior and ask Him to bring it to you.

I have to confess I could never have envisioned the gift spiritual friendship would bring to my life. I am blessed beyond measure to be part of a group of six women that started studying personal leadership together, only to have God lead us to one another in spiritual friendship. Through the years, they have taught me, challenged me, encouraged me, and prayed tirelessly for me and my family. We have an uncommon bond. We can text or call at any time, knowing we have each other's backs (and hearts). We have a saying we use when we are requesting intense prayer for a particular person or circumstance in our lives. We simply say, "Shields Up" as a picture that represents us standing shoulder to shoulder in a circle, our backs pressed against each other, our shields raised heavenward and locked in place. That phrase is our cue to pray passionately and fervently about the matter at hand. Their spiritual friendship has contributed significantly to the guarding of my heart and its ability to live at rest.

Key Learnings:

❤ Spiritual friendship is doing life together on a heart level
❤ Spiritual friendship is not a program; it is a relationship
❤ Spiritual friendship is not a mentor/mentee relationship; the learning goes both ways.
❤ Spiritual friendship requires our ability to receive from God and others.
❤ The value of a spiritual friend is not always that they teach you something new, but rather that they remind you of things that you already know. They may even give you the last 10%.

Passages to Ponder:

"Two are better than one, because they have a good return for their labor: If either of them falls down, one can help the other up. But pity anyone who falls and has no one to help them up" (Ecclesiastes 4:9-10).

"Can two people walk together without agreeing on the direction?" (Amos 3:3).

"One who has unreliable friends soon comes to ruin, but there is a friend who sticks closer than a brother" (Proverbs 18:24 NIV).

"Do not forsake your friend or a friend of your family, and do not go to your relative's house when disaster strikes you—better a neighbor nearby than a relative far away" (Proverbs 27:10).

Questions to Consider:

1. What barriers to spiritual friendship are currently in your life?

2.   What do you need to do to remove them?

3.   What are some first steps you can take to move toward meaningful spiritual relationships?

4.   Who is the person that God is prompting you to explore a possible spiritual friendship?

Prayer of Invitation:

Almighty God,
Thank You that it has always been Your plan for us to live in community and not try and go it alone. Open my heart and mind to the potential spiritual friendship holds for me. Teach me how to receive from You and from others. Guide me to the person(s) of Your choosing, in Your time and in Your way. By Your grace, may I also be a good spiritual friend to someone else who needs one. Forge those friendships by Your Spirit, I pray. Amen.

Practice Point:

Set a recurring reminder on your phone each day for the next month to remind you to pray for God's direction in pursuing spiritual friendship. Set it for a time that is separate from your regular prayer time. Pray specifically that God would:
- prepare your heart to be a spiritual friend
- be preparing the heart of your future spiritual friend
- connect you at just the right time.

Chapter 12

The Sacred Heart: Finding God to Be More Than Enough

As we come to the close of the book, I trust you've been able to identify some life principles that will support you as you move toward living with your heart at rest. Notice I said, *living* with your heart at rest, not merely existing. Living with your heart at rest is not a static concept, it is dynamic. It becomes part of who you are as you move through life. It reflects the decision of your mind, your will and your emotions to function under a new MO. (Modus Operandi) The principles and strategies that we've discussed will be helpful in moving you toward greater peace in your life, but in and of themselves, they are powerless on their own (or even as a collective group) to bring your heart to a place of rest. It's a lot like washing your hair with a high-quality shampoo. Everything is clean and it even smells really good, but without a good conditioner, your hair is still knotted up. The same is true in our spiritual lives. We may be doing all the right things—maintaining high levels of integrity, engaging in numerous spiritual disciplines, and even have a reputation for being godly and wise; but, without the conditioning of the Holy Spirit, our internal lives will still be knotted up. They will remain dry, limp and/or frizzy. (I have naturally curly hair, so I understand the need for conditioning well.)

Just as conditioner brings shine, clarity, resilience, and definition to our hair, that's what the Holy Spirit brings to the whole of our lives when we surrender to His conditioning. He brings life, health, and an unexplainable sparkle to our entire existence when we allow His conditioning work to take root in our lives. While conditioner brings a silky smoothness to our hair, the Holy Spirit's work in our lives brings a soft, tenderness to our spirit that is reflected in how we live out our lives. A good conditioner untangles hair that got gnarled up in the cleaning process, and restores its ph level (balance between acidity and alkalinity) allowing its natural beauty to shine through. Similarly, the Holy Spirit brings the proper balance to our lives and helps restore our hearts to God's original design and intention. The conditioning work of the Holy Spirit is what enables us to live with our hearts at rest.

I believe that journey of conditioning our heart all starts with an intentional choice on our part to pursue the renewing of our mind. This is hard work, and I remind you once again that if this was easy, more people would do it and do it well. "The mind is the last frontier. By the time you're ready to invite God to take authority over your thought life, you're serious."[64] Romans 12:2 teaches us that we will act different when we think different. "Don't copy the behavior and customs of this world, but let God transform you into a new person by changing the way you think. Then you will learn to know God's will for you, which is good and pleasing and perfect." The transformation that our hearts are hungry for will only happen as we *choose* to invest the time we need to sit with our Savior so that He can bring about the necessary changes in our thought life. "Working on our thought lives is the only thing that will keep them from working on us. Either our thoughts have control of us through the power of the enemy or we have control of them through the power of God. Neutral doesn't exist among the mental gears. That doesn't mean rest doesn't exist... Re-wallpapering (the walls of our mind) is hard work, but rest comes as we learn to abide in what we know."[65]

Ephesians 4:22-23 instructs us to "throw off your old, evil nature and your former way of life, which is ... full of lust and deception.

Instead, there must be a spiritual renewal of your thoughts and attitudes." How does that happen? We've all tried to develop strategies to deal with the issues of life only to come up short and be frustrated. We cannot live with our hearts at rest by sheer will power alone. Trying to do so is exactly that, trying to "do" God's job. Contrary to the thinking of our culture, rather than letting our thoughts and emotions rule us, we need to spur them in the right direction. Scripture is clear on the battle in our minds and the impact that battle has on our souls. "The mind governed by the flesh is death, but the mind governed by the Spirit is life and peace" (Romans 8:6 NIV). It's all about feeding our spirit and starving our flesh. (sinful nature). Which ever thought process gets the most time and attention will have the upper hand in our lives.

But God does not leave us defenseless. "The weapons we fight with are not the weapons of the world. On the contrary, they have divine power to demolish strongholds. We demolish arguments and every pretension that sets itself up against the knowledge of God, and we take captive every thought to make it obedient to Christ" (2 Corinthians 10:4-5). We take our thoughts captive and bring them into obedience to Christ when we sit with our Savior, linger with our Lord and let Him do what only He can do, as we still our minds and hearts in His presence. I honestly don't understand *how* God brings about the spiritual renewal of our thoughts and attitudes, but I'm so grateful that He does. Paul provides some perspective in 1 Corinthians 1:18-19, "For the message of the cross is foolishness to those who are perishing, but to us who are being saved it is the power of God. For it is written: 'I will destroy the wisdom of the wise; the intelligence of the intelligent I will frustrate.'" God knows that we don't always understand His ways or how we should live them out. That's why He wants us to come to Him and ask Him for His wisdom. "If you need wisdom, ask our generous God, and He will give it to you. He will not rebuke you for asking" (James 1:5). One translation of the Bible reminds us that God "gives to all men liberally" (KJV). Notice the words, "generous" and "liberally." God is not stingy with His wisdom, He is waiting for us to ask for it.

By now you know that I love acronyms. They help me organize my thoughts and remember key concepts. I want to leave you with two short acronyms that I believe encapsulate the bulk of the material discussed in this book. Since their inception in my mind several years ago, I have yet to encounter a situation or circumstance where their counsel did not bring direction, encouragement, or perspective. While they have no special power in and of themselves, they have become faithful companions on my journey through life.

S.A.M.

Show me truth.

Align my will.

Make Your way clear.

Show Me Truth

Begin by asking for wisdom. Whenever we encounter a situation or circumstance where we don't know what to do or we know there is something our minds and hearts can't seem to grasp, we need to ask God to show us truth. Truth about ourselves, truth about our circumstances, truth about the other person (if applicable), and truth about Himself and His character. "God's Word is your truth serum. The more you use it, the clearer your mind will become."[66] When we think, believe and apply biblical truth as a lifestyle, God's promised rest takes over. That's why knowing His Word is so crucial to experiencing rest. "All your words are true; all your righteous laws are eternal" (Psalm 119:160). "Sanctify them by the truth; your word is truth" (John 17:17 NIV). Knowing the power and authority that God's Word contains, this was Jesus' prayer for His disciples and for His followers down through the centuries. He understood the ability of Scripture to consecrate us, to make us holy. Soaking in God's truth marinates our hearts with wisdom so we can better understand His ways and submit to His sovereignty.

God's Word is able to discern "the thoughts and intents of our heart" (Hebrews 4:12). It is a divine mirror for our souls. It helps us see where our thinking is incongruent—like when we spend too freely and then wonder why God isn't providing like we think He should. Or when we speak too quickly or too harshly and then find our relationships aren't as fulfilling as we'd hoped. Or when we try to disguise our self-serving motives as something different than what they really are. It exposes our duplicity when we are living in direct defiance to God's Word and then wonder why we aren't experiencing His hand of blessing and favor.

God's Word helps us to better understand other people and their perspective. The Apostle Paul provides a biblical explanation to the human dilemma. "I don't really understand myself, for I want to do what is right, but I don't do it. Instead, I do what I hate. But if I know that what I am doing is wrong, this shows that I agree that the law is good. So I am not the one doing wrong; it is sin living in me that does it. And I know that nothing good lives in me, that is, in my sinful nature. I want to do what is right, but I can't. I want to do what is good, but I don't. I don't want to do what is wrong, but I do it anyway" (Romans 7:15-19). This quandary is not unique to you or to me. It pervades mankind and offers insight into the actions of the 'other' people in our lives. "By His divine power, God has given us everything we need for living a godly life" (2 Peter 1:3). Part of the "everything" we need includes grace. God intended for grace to be a significant part of our experience here on earth. Extending it and receiving it. If any human could *get it right* down here, we wouldn't need Jesus, we wouldn't need grace and there would be no need to go to heaven. God understands our struggle with sin, self-sufficiency, and pride so He designed grace. Grace was His idea! "Well then, should we keep on sinning so that God can show us more and more of His wonderful grace?" (Romans 6:1). Clearly not. Grace is not a license for spiritual apathy or an excuse for spiritual laziness but rather God's loving response to our human nature. He knows "we are but dust" (Psalm 103:14) and that while "the spirit is willing, the flesh is weak" (Matthew 26:41).

God's Word reveals His heart and character. There are many passages in Scripture that speak of Who God is and what He is like but I am particularly drawn to Psalm 103. As you read it, observe our heart's response when we begin to grasp all that God does for us and how deeply He cares about us.

"Let all that I am praise the LORD; with my whole heart, I will praise his holy name. Let all that I am praise the LORD; may I never forget the good things he does for me. He forgives all my sins and heals all my diseases. He redeems me from death and crowns me with love and tender mercies. He fills my life with good things. My youth is renewed like the eagle's! The LORD gives righteousness and justice to all who are treated unfairly. He revealed his character to Moses and his deeds to the people of Israel. The LORD is compassionate and merciful, slow to get angry and filled with unfailing love. He will not constantly accuse us, nor remain angry forever. He does not punish us for all our sins; he does not deal harshly with us, as we deserve. For his unfailing love toward those who fear him is as great as the height of the heavens above the earth. He has removed our sins as far from us as the east is from the west. The LORD is like a father to his children, tender and compassionate to those who fear him. For he knows how weak we are; he remembers we are only dust. Our days on earth are like grass; like wildflowers, we bloom and die. The wind blows, and we are gone— as though we had never been here. But the love of the LORD remains forever with those who fear him. His salvation extends to the children's children of those who are faithful to his covenant, of those who obey his commandments! The LORD has made the heavens his throne; from there he rules over everything. Praise the LORD, you angels, you mighty ones who carry out his plans, listening for each of his commands. Yes, praise the LORD, you armies of angels who serve him and do his will! Praise the LORD, everything he has created, everything in all his kingdom. Let all that I am praise the LORD."

When we catch a glimpse of the magnitude and compassion of Almighty God, our heart's reflex is to worship. I believe that's why Psalm 92:1 instructs us, "It is good to give thanks to the LORD, to sing praises to the Most High." Worship plays a key role in bringing and sustaining our hearts at a place of rest. "We were created to worship God. It's a state in which our soul finds true peace, rest and purpose. But it must become a condition of the heart, a way of life, a pattern woven into the fabric of our being."[67]

"We do not worship God to *obtain* His blessings. That's not really worshiping *God*; that's worshiping the *blessings*. But whenever we fully acknowledge who God is and worship Him as such, our praise unleashes the blessings that are *with* Him and *in* Him and *because* of Him."[68]

Align My Will

If you consider the kinds of prayers that most of us pray, they are, at their core, usually a request for comfort, control, or blessing. *Lord, please take away the pain. Please don't let this happen in my life or my family's life. Please bless our efforts.* That is our way of thinking. We don't always see purpose in pain or even in the mundane, but God does. That's why we need to pray as the psalmist did, "Teach me Your ways, O LORD, that I may live according to Your truth! Grant me purity of heart, so that I may honor You" (Psalm 86:11).

Sometimes we need to pray and ask God, "Help me want Your agenda more than my own." Other times, we need to ask Him to change our *want to*. And then there are times when we honestly don't know how to feel about a situation, so it is necessary to invite Him to bring our will into alignment with His. Once again, it's about the posture of our hearts—aligning them in submission and surrender, choosing God's way over our own. Undoubtedly, there are times when choosing God's way over ours may seem difficult, if not impossible to do, but God promises His strength to those who desire to live His way. "The eyes of the LORD search the whole earth in order to strengthen those whose hearts are fully committed to Him" (2 Chronicles 16:9). Proverbs 3:5,6 provides timeless instruction, "Trust in the LORD with **all** your heart; do not depend on your own understanding. Seek His will in all you do, and He will show you which path to take" [Emphasis Mine]. Notice the verse says *all* your heart, not just half of it. A half-hearted approach to surrender will always leave you feeling disillusioned and victimized by God. By way of reminder, the degree to which you trust God will be the degree to which your experience rest for your soul. Psalm 91:1 teaches us that, "Those who *live* in the shelter of the Most High will find rest in the shadow of the Almighty" [Emphasis Mine]. We learn to trust Him by doing life *with* Him, conscious of His presence with us, inviting Him into the moments of our life.

Make Your Way Clear

In Psalm 32:8 we read God's promise of direction for our lives. "I will guide you along the best pathway for your life. I will advise you and watch over you." Throughout Scripture, we read of those who petitioned God for His guidance, "Lead me O Lord, in Your righteousness…make your way straight before my face" (Psalm 5:8). And then there are those who testify to God's faithfulness in following through on His promise. "You make known to me the path of life; You will fill me with joy in your presence, with eternal pleasures at Your right hand" (Psalm 16:11 NIV). Whenever we are seeking God's guidance, Psalm 119:105 provides us with our first step, "Your word is a lamp to guide my feet and a light for my path." Starting our search for direction and clarity in God's Word protects us from our own agenda and the misguided wisdom of the world. Knowing my own propensity to prematurely move to strategy and action, quickly breezing past God's desired plans and purposes, I often pray, "Lord Jesus, make Your way so clear that I can't miss it."

Staying on PAR in Life

I'm not a golfer but the concepts contained in this last acronym have kept me out of the *sand traps* of life and helped me stay on PAR amidst the storms and struggles.

Pour out your pain.

Agree with the Almighty (that He has the right to orchestrate the events of your life).

Receive all He has for you.

Pour Out Your Pain

We've already talked about this in great length earlier, so let me just provide a few brief statements of reminder. It's important to pour out our pain to God, not just to others. As cathartic as pouring out our pain to others may feel, real transformation takes place when we bring our pain to God. "O my people, trust in Him at all times, pour out your pain to Him, for God is our refuge" (Psalm 62:8). Suppressing our hurt in hopes that it will heal over time just adds to the pressure that builds inside of us. The schedules of counselors and psychologists are filled with those who have tried to hide or ignore their pain, only to have it resurface in unexpected and unwanted ways. There's no getting around it. If we don't deal with our pain now, it *will* show up at another less opportune time and in much less desirable way than we'd like. The price for our pride and resistance in this area is steep and unrelenting. As always, Scripture provides the remedy, "So humble yourselves before God. Resist the devil, and he will flee from you. Come close to God, and God will come close to you. Wash your hands, you sinners; purify your hearts, for your loyalty is divided between God and the world … Humble yourselves before the Lord, and he will lift you up in honor" (James 4:7,8,10). The vulnerability we express to Him as we pour out our pain takes our relationship to new heights where new levels of peace can be found.

Agree with the Almighty (that He has the right to orchestrate the events of your life)

We focused on surrendering to God's sovereignty earlier so again, I just want to highlight a few key points. Perhaps you've wrestled with God and have surrendered some of the bigger issues in your life to His control, but what about the day-to-day happenings of your life? Are you really OK with God allowing or not allowing things to happen to us in your everyday life? What about relationship struggles and those prickly people in your life?

Agreeing with the Almighty requires ongoing submission. Even though I have submitted to God's sovereignty concerning our son's diagnosis of Cerebral Palsy, the day-to-day living out of that major decision still requires countless comparatively minor, but nonetheless important choices to yield to God's will and way. For all of us, it is the embodiment of Galatians 2:20, "I am crucified with Christ, I myself no longer live, but Christ lives in me. So I live my life in this earthly body by trusting in the Son of God, who loved me and gave himself for me." It also requires ongoing repentance. By God's grace, we can take some significant strides forward in our desire to submit to His sovereignty and live with our hearts at rest, but we will still blow it from time to time. We will make a poor choice, lose patience, or get overwhelmed and discouraged. Repentance is the only way back to the *highway of holiness* (Isaiah 35:8) after our sin detour. Without it, God no longer responds to our requests for direction (Psalm 66:18).

When we understand that enormity of God's wisdom and power, we begin to understand that He is always up to 1000 more things than the obvious. That's why He reminds us in Isaiah that, "My ways are not your ways and My thoughts are not your thoughts…" (Isaiah 55:8). From our limited vantage point, what initially seems bad might indeed end up being very good and conversely what at first glance seems good may turn out to be just the opposite.

In her book *Jesus Always,* Sarah Young writes in the first person, as if Jesus were speaking to us one on one. She writes, "Be willing to follow My lead, beloved. Open yourself more fully to Me and My way for you. Don't get so focused on what you want that you miss the things I've prepared for you…. Sometimes you obstruct the very things you desire by trying too hard to make things go according to your will and timing. I know the desires of your heart, and I also know the best way to reach those goals. Instead of striving to be in control so you can get what you want, seek My face."[69] Jesus' actual words in Matthew 10:39 are much more succinct and exacting, "If you cling to your life, you will lose it; but if you give it up for me, you will find it."

Receive All He Has for You

Often, there is a lot of focus, and rightfully so, on what we lose when we cling to our agenda for our lives, but considerably less attention is given to what we find or gain when we surrender to God's will and way. I believe that is why many of us are hesitant to yield to God's plans for our life. We really don't comprehend what awaits us, not just in eternity, but in the here and now. Somehow, we have come to grossly underestimate and diminish the value of God's presence. Perhaps, it's because we don't really understand its power. Or we don't believe that it will make that much of a difference. Either way, living outside of God's presence makes it impossible for us to live with our hearts at rest. We are left feeling frustrated, forgotten, and left to fend for ourselves in a world that cares little about our heart or its ability to live at rest. A dark place indeed. *But God. I love that phrase. But God!* But God made a way for things to be so much better. He sent the Holy Spirit to "abide and to take up residence" in our hearts. "And we know he lives in us because the Spirit he gave us lives in us" (1 John 3:24). Because God by His Spirit lives within us, He calls us to a much better way to live. A life that invites Him into our moments so we can experience the gift of His enduring existence in our lives. He wants us to recognize His attentiveness to our needs, not just physical, but also mental, emotional, and spiritual. He wants to anchor our souls with the peace "which is far more wonderful than the human mind can understand" (Philippians 4:6). Even though we don't understand it, doesn't mean it's not real. He wants us to enjoy and be empowered by the day-to-day, boots-on-the-ground experience of Emmanuel (God with us). Doing life with God, conscious of His presence, is the ultimate game-changer in our heart's ability to live at rest. It is what allows you to fall back to sleep at night knowing that not only is He willing and more than able to supply whatever is needed to address the concerns replaying in your mind, but also that He will be *with* you, no matter what happens. It's knowing that you will never have to walk into any situation, whether it be a doctor's office, a court room, or into the funeral of someone you love and have to wait for God to arrive. He will already be there, waiting for you, saying "_____(insert your name), I'm here, take my hand, let's do this together."

"I will never leave you or forsake you" (Hebrews 13:5 KJV). Being aware of His presence takes away that lingering sense of fear and foreboding that something bad is about to happen in your life. "In the multitude of my anxieties within me, Your comforts delight my soul" (Psalm 94:19 NKJV). It answers the question, "Is God good when … ?" because you will have experienced His goodness in the power of His presence. We have bought into the lie that rest for our hearts only comes when God rescues us from our current struggle. Rest is not inextricably linked to our rescue; it rises up when we recognize the power His presence brings to our lives. "Don't be afraid, for I am *with* you. Do not be dismayed for I am your God. I will strengthen you. I will help you. I will uphold you with my victorious right hand" (Isaiah 41:10)[Emphasis Mine].

In the Old Testament, we read countless times of how God was *with* His people—*with* Abraham, *with* Moses, *with* Samuel, *with* David, *with* Esther, *with* Hannah, *with, with, with* … and *comprehending* the significance of God being *with* them changed the direction of their lives. It shifted the posture of their hearts. It's what allowed them to not only do uncommon feats, but it also provided the inner strength and fortitude they needed to live with their hearts at rest despite their circumstances. Of the many examples Scripture provides, please consider the following:

Jacob

In Genesis 28:15, as Jacob is fleeing his homeland, God tells him, "I will be *with* you, and I will protect you wherever you go. I will someday bring you safely back to this land. I will be *with* you constantly until I have finished giving you everything I have promised" [Emphasis Mine]. Then several years later God instructs him to "return to the land of your father…and I will be *with* you." [Emphasis Mine]. Toward the end of his life, God directs him to "Go down to Egypt ... I will go *with* you" (Genesis 46:3,4) [Emphasis Mine]. Notice God does not tell Jacob to go anywhere alone. He assured him that He would go with him. The promise of God's presence gave Jacob the courage and strength to leave his homeland, endure betrayal from a family member (which resulted in him having to work 14 years for the woman he loved), and then return home to a potentially life-threatening situation with his estranged brother. God understands the *slop* of our lives. He understands family drama and when His presence intersects with our reality, it has a powerful effect. By His Spirit, God's promise to be *with* Jacob extends to us today.

Joseph

"The Lord was *with* Joseph and blessed him greatly as he served in the home of his Egyptian master" (Genesis 39:2) [Emphasis Mine]. Despite being sold into slavery by his brothers, things seemed to be going quite well for Joseph... until he was falsely accused and thrown into prison. "But the Lord was *with* Joseph there, too, and He granted Joseph favor with the chief jailer" (Genesis 39:21) [Emphasis Mine]. Stephen retells Joseph's story in Act 7:9,10 noting that "These sons of Jacob were very jealous of their brother Joseph, and they sold him to be a slave in Egypt. But God was *with* him and delivered him out of his anguish" [Emphasis Mine]. It was 13 years from the time Joseph was first sold into slavery until he was exonerated and released from prison. Thirteen years is a long time. Consider the power of God's presence to sustain Joseph through betrayal, false accusations, unjust treatment, and plain old discouragement. Yet, Genesis 50:20 records his statement of surrender to God's sovereignty, as shared with his brothers. "You intended to harm me, but God intended it for good to accomplish what is now being done, the saving of many lives" (NIV).

Joshua

In the first chapter of the book of Joshua we read that Moses, the only leader the Israelite people had ever known, had died, leaving Joshua tasked with leading the nation of Israel into the

Promised Land. The Israelites had demonstrated their rebellion and ingratitude enough times through the years for Joshua to realize that his biggest leadership challenge may not be conquering the enemy nations ahead. Rather, instilling confidence in the people, allaying their fears, rallying their commitment to go to battle, and overcoming internal resistance may prove to be the more arduous tasks. While we might only be able to imagine the anxiety rising up in Joshua's heart, God knew it well so He promised him, "I will be *with* you as I was with Moses. I will not fail you or abandon you" (Joshua 1:6). Read the counsel God gives Joshua in the next two verses and see if you don't recognize some familiar principles, "Be strong and courageous, for you will lead my people to possess all the land I swore to give their ancestors. Be strong and very courageous. Obey all the laws Moses gave you. Do not turn away from them, and you will be successful in everything you do. Study this book of the Law continually. Meditate on it day and night so you may be sure to obey all that is written in it. Only then will you succeed. I command you – be strong and courageous! Do not be afraid or discouraged. For the Lord your God is *with* you wherever you go" (Joshua 1:7-9). Obedience, reading God's Word, choosing to believe God's promises, and recognizing the importance and implications of God's presence are all core ingredients that enable us to live with our heart at rest.

David

David's life was wrought with a roller coaster of victorious highs and humiliating lows. We read in 1 Samuel 18:14 of his military prowess, "David continued to succeed in everything he did, for the Lord was *with* him" [Emphasis Mine]. Then after his sin with Bathsheba, we hear him imploring the Lord, "Do not banish me from your presence and don't take your Holy Spirit from me" (Psalm 51:11). Our lives may not have all the extraordinary extremes that David's did, but it is clear from the above passage that he understood well the importance of God's presence in the extreme and the routine happenings of his life. Reflect on David's comprehension of all that God's presence brought into his life as you read this familiar passage with fresh eyes.

"The LORD is my shepherd; I have all that I need. He lets me rest in green meadows; He leads me beside peaceful streams. He renews my strength. He guides me along right paths, bringing honor to His name. Even when I walk through the darkest valley, I will not be afraid, for You are close beside me. Your rod and Your staff protect and comfort me. You prepare a feast for me in the presence of my enemies. You honor me by anointing my head with oil. My cup overflows with blessings. Surely your goodness and unfailing love will pursue me all the days of my life, and I will live in the house of the LORD forever" (Psalm 23).

Peace, protection, provision, direction, deliverance, honor, blessings, hope, love, and security.

They are all found in His presence. This passage serves to realign our thinking so that we can see that the impact of God's presence on our life is all about Who *He* is and what *He* does, not who we are or what we do. Living with our heart at rest is all about recognizing the power of God's presence and letting it shift the posture of our heart. Our thoughts then have a new perspective from which to draw, which in turn changes our actions. "You will keep in perfect peace all who trust in you, whose thoughts are fixed on you" (Isaiah 26:3). When our thoughts are focused on Jesus, they are focused on His wisdom and power and not our own. When our thoughts are fixed on Him, the questions of "why?" and "why me?" begin to melt away. Despite our best attempts to figure our lives out, "knowing the answers will not give us the peace we want. *Knowing the Lord is what will give us peace.*"[70]

Perhaps you noticed that in none of the biblical examples cited did God rescue the people from their hardship, at least not right away. Rather, He met them in their moments and journeyed *with* them through their circumstance. He entered their world and allowed His presence to transfer the focus off of their problems and onto His power to encourage, redeem and provide what was needed. When God's presence floods our lives, despair gives way to hope, anxiety melts into peace, fear loses its grip, and joy begins to make itself at home in our hearts. I wish I could sit across the table from you and look you right in the eyes and tell you how I know, that I know that I know that this is true. When I could see no way out from the chaos swirling in my heart and mind, pausing to invite Christ into my moments opened the door for Him to steady my heart and focus my mind. "I call as my heart grows faint, lead me to the rock that is higher than I" (Psalm 61:2 NIV). Another translation says, "My heart is overwhelmed, lead me to the towering rock of safety" (NLT).

Christ understood well the value of His Father's presence. Scripture provides virtually no record of Jesus' response to physical pain but chronicles His anguished cry at being separated from the Father. It's important to note that God the Father never *rescued* Christ from the cross. As agonizing as it was for the Father to watch His Son in excruciating pain, He accomplished something much greater by choosing not to remove the suffering.

When the posture of our heart resists God's best path for our lives (even when that includes pain), the avenue through which God pours Himself into our lives becomes clogged and our view of life and of God becomes distorted. Remember, as God is, so life is. On the other hand, when we adopt a posture of heart that embraces God's sovereign plan with humility, it serves to remove the kinks and other obstructions blocking the way so that His power, love, and grace can flow freely into our lives. If we truly understood what it would be like to have these blessings flowing freely in our lives, I believe we would be much more motivated to live a surrendered life. In Luke 11:13, Jesus tells us that. "If you then, being evil, know how to give good gifts to your children, how much more will your heavenly Father give the Holy Spirit to those who ask Him!" Once again, we see that God is not unwilling to share Himself and the blessings that are intrinsic to His character. On the contrary, He desires to bring Who He is to bear on our lives. David proclaims in Psalm 61:5 that, "You have given me the heritage of those who fear your name" and declares again in Psalm 16:5-6, "Lord, You alone are my inheritance, my cup of blessing, You guard all that is mine. The land You have given me is a pleasant land. What a wonderful inheritance!" While many of us may like the idea of an inheritance, the concept of how that translates into our daily life remains elusive "unless you can forever settle in your heart that you are a true son or daughter of God."[71] John 1:12 confirms that, "to all who believed Him and accepted Him, He gave the right to become the children of God." If you have accepted Christ as your personal Savior, you are God's child, and He wants you to receive all that He has made available to you. "Once you settle this issue, and come to know God as *your* heavenly Father, your life will change. You'll begin to take on a family resemblance. You will have your Father's eyes, heart and mind."[72]

It starts with an act of our will. "If we never take the first step of pure faith and obey, we'll never realize we can trust."[73] God does not expect us to have everything in order before we respond to His invitation. He invites us to come with our burdens and weariness. "Then Jesus said, 'Come to Me, all of you who are weary and carry heavy burdens, and I will give you rest. Take my yoke upon you. Let me teach you, because I am humble and gentle, and you will find rest for your souls. For my yoke fits perfectly, and the burden I give you is light.'" This is a familiar passage and it's easy to skip over its significance. The humility and courage required to bring the "stuff of our lives" to God and let Him teach us His ways are not common but they do produce uncommon results. You may feel that the time it takes to sit with your Savior is unproductive and of little value. That's what people thought about the woman named Mary when she anointed Jesus' feet with expensive perfume. She desired to express her gratitude for the forgiveness He had extended to her, but she also did not want to miss out on all that Jesus had for her. Jesus defended her choice and in the process of simply sitting at His feet, she became a recipient of the beauty of that anointing aroma (John 12:3).

Colossians 2:6-7 provides clear direction on how we receive all Christ died to provide for us, "And now, just as you accepted Christ Jesus as your Lord, you must continue to live in obedience to Him. Let your roots grow down into Him and draw up nourishment from Him, so you will grow in faith, strong and vigorous in the truth you were taught. Let your lives overflow with thanksgiving for all He has done for you." Scripture is replete with the pattern for living with our heart at rest and we see it again in this passage—obedience/submission, sitting with our Savior, and worship. This combination will allow us to "draw up the nourishment" our souls hunger for. When we do, we will be able to say with the Psalmist, "My soul finds rest in God alone" (Psalm 62:5).

Journey vs Destination

Living with your heart at rest is not a destination for arrival some day. Until the day God calls us home, living with our heart at rest is an ongoing spiritual journey that mourns what was lost in the Garden of Eden—unceasing, unencumbered communion with Almighty God. It is also a journey that looks forward to the glorious restoration of that relationship. As we live in that tension between what once was and what will one day be, God desires to walk *with* us and share Himself *with* us, for as our Creator, He knows that we were created to be incomplete without Him.

As we talked about earlier, our life's journey is seldom, if ever, a straight line. It is filled with twists, curves, and many steep inclines. We desperately need God's guidance to lead the way, knowing that whatever path He takes us on, it will always be one that leads us back to Him.

Our faith and choice to trust God completely is like the blood in our bodies. We need it to keep moving and circulating in our bodies in order for us to survive. The heart pumps oxygenated blood out of our physical hearts to every part of our body, but then the blood needs to return to its source, to get re-oxygenated in order for it to continue to be of value. If our blood did not return to our heart and lungs to get a fresh supply of oxygen, it would pump bad blood through our system and render our bodies useless to function as designed. Disease and malfunction would set in and our entire body would be forced to exist in a state of chaos. The only thing that keeps our bodies from self-destructing is our blood getting back to its life-giving source. In our physical bodies, most of that journey back to the heart is uphill.

So it is with our spiritual hearts. The daily difficulties and demands that come as part of our human existence suck the life out of our spirits. We need to routinely go back to the Source so that He can anchor our souls and fill us with His peace. Our lifeblood's value is in its ability to sustain us as we move through life. Our faith is only valuable when it is meaningful and addresses the real issues of our life. Jesus reassures us that on our journey through life, He not only understands the lay of the land, He guarantees that His power and presence can successfully navigate us through the struggle and back to the heart of God. "I have told you these things, so that in me you may have peace. In this world, you will have trouble. But take heart! I have overcome the world" (John 16:33 NIV).

Dear friends, I leave you with the words of an old hymn by William J. Kirkpatrick,

'Tis So Sweet To Trust in Jesus

'Tis so sweet to trust in Jesus, just to take
Him at His Word.
Just to rest upon His promise, Just to know,
'thus saith the Lord.
Jesus, Jesus, how I trust Him! **How I've
proved Him o'er and o'er**
Jesus, Jesus, precious Jesus! **O for grace to
trust Him more!**[74]

May your heart find rest as you learn to trust Him more.

"The LORD is my strength and my shield; my heart trusts in him, and he helps me. My heart leaps for joy, and with my song I praise him" (Psalm 28:7).

Key Learnings:

- ❤ The conditioning work of the Holy Spirit is what enables us to live with our hearts at rest.
- ❤ A half-hearted approach to surrender will always leave you feeling disillusioned and victimized by God.
- ❤ When we truly understand the implications of God being *with* us, we find His presence to be more than enough.
- ❤ S.A.M. Show me truth. Align My Will. Make Your way clear.
- ❤ PAR - Pour out your pain. Agree with the Almighty. Receive All He has for you.

Passages to Ponder:

"Don't copy the behavior and customs of this world, but let God transform you into a new person by changing the way you think. Then you will learn to know God's will for you, which is good and pleasing and perfect" (Romans 12:2).

"The mind governed by the flesh is death, but the mind governed by the Spirit is life and peace" (Romans 8:6 NIV).

"The weapons we fight with are not the weapons of the world. On the contrary, they have divine power to demolish strongholds. We demolish arguments and every pretension that sets itself up against the knowledge of God, and we take captive every thought to make it obedient to Christ" (2 Corinthians 10:4-5 NIV).

"Rather, it was simply that the LORD loves you, and he was keeping the oath he had sworn to your ancestors. That is why the LORD rescued you with such a strong hand from your slavery and from the oppressive hand of Pharaoh, king of Egypt. Understand, therefore, that the LORD your God is indeed God. He is the faithful God who keeps his covenant for a thousand generations and lavishes his unfailing love on those who love him and obey his commands" (Deuteronomy 7:8-9).

"Now you have every spiritual gift you need as you eagerly wait for the return of our Lord Jesus Christ. He will keep you strong to the end so that you will be free from all blame on the day when our Lord Jesus Christ returns. God will do this, for he is faithful to do what he says, and he has invited you into partnership with his Son, Jesus Christ our Lord" (1 Corinthians 1:7-9).

Prayer of Invitation:

O Lord Jesus,
Praise You that You not only redeem and restore me, You also want to 'do life' with me.
I invite the conditioning work of the Holy Spirit into my life.
I want Your unexplainable sparkle over my entire existence.
Show me truth. Align my will. Make Your way clear. In the matchless name of Jesus, I pray. Amen.

Practice Point:

We end back where we started—in the shower! Buy a good quality hair conditioner and as you apply it to your hair, ask the Holy Spirit to apply His conditioning to your heart. As you massage the conditioner through your hair, reflect on all the ways God has massaged your heart as we have journeyed together. Thank Him that He not only cleanses your heart but He also restores its natural beauty and shine. Praise Him for what is yet to come!

Appendix

Greatest Fears of the Personality Types

Closely tied to our emotional needs are our greatest fears. I believe the list below provides some obvious correlations.

Popular Sanguine – going unnoticed, blending in; being alone, getting old, ugly, unpopular or ignored.

Perfect Melancholy – not getting everything right; being misunderstood.

Powerful Choleric – losing control – of family, job or health; all of these indicate failure or weakness.

Peaceful Phlegmatic – being pressured to work all the time; left *holding the bag*; having to deal with overwhelming conflict.

Addictive Natures of the Personality Types

As distinctive as each person is in how they respond to stress, especially prolonged stress, there are some commonalities within each of the personality types that can also be linked back to their respective emotional needs.

Popular Sanguine – people wired like this are most likely to engage in substance abuse when life is no fun, due to prolonged hardship or lack of social interaction. They can be prone to addiction to fun, food, shopping, relationships, and romance, so their response to stress is to go shopping, party with friends, eat to cheer up, and find a way to reward themselves.

Perfect Melancholy – folks with this personality are most likely to reach for alcohol or drugs when life seems out of control with no hope of them being able to bring it back to center. Given their tendencies to be addicted to perfection, neatness, and solitude, their response to prolonged stress often is to withdraw from people, read, study, meditate, and isolate themselves from others.

Powerful Choleric – given their need for control, these folks are prone to engage in substance abuse when they have problems with money, their mate, their children, their job, or their health that they can't control. That urge also arises when they feel totally unappreciated. They are often addicted to work, control, exercise, and power and so their strategy is to work harder, exercise more, and stay away from unyielding situations (people).

Peaceful Phlegmatic – folks who are wired this way are most likely to reach for alcohol or drugs when life seems full of conflict and chaos, when they know they should confront a situation but are avoiding it or when they feel pressured to produce. Their drugs of choice tend to be TV, technology, food, spectator sports, and sleep, so when they feel perpetually overwhelmed, their response is to engage in any or all of the above in an attempt to tune out on life.

Mechanisms of Control

Whenever life seems out of control or not going the way they want it to, each of the personality types has a *go to* mechanism for trying to bring things back into their preferred way of doing life. The **Popular Sanguine** uses charm and wit to sway you to their way of thinking while the **Perfect Melancholy** tries to manipulate using his/her moods (i.e. sulking, withdrawing). The **Powerful Choleric's** weapon of choice is anger and is often accompanied by them wagging his/her pointer finger in your face. The **Peaceful Phlegmatic** wields a less aggressive but equally dangerous weapon in an attempt to maintain control, and that is procrastination. "If the Spirit isn't moving, then they aren't either." (and even if the Spirit *is* moving, sometimes they still aren't!)

Learned Behaviors & Blended Personality Types

At this point, I feel like a note of further caution/instruction is warranted. For some of you, it may have been easy to identify your personality type, and the temptation is to move on and start analyzing others which can lead to putting them in a box. Please resist that temptation. For others, you may be struggling, thinking, "well, sometimes I'm like one personality and sometimes I'm like another one, maybe even seemingly opposite ones." Let me clarify a few things. First of all, no one is typically 100% one personality type to the exclusion of others. We are a unique blend. Secondly, your work or family circumstances may require you to operate outside of your God-given personality type. Doing this is exhausting and often the source of much frustration and anxiety. Try to think of who you are barefoot, who you are when you're by yourself with no outside demands on you. That should give you better insight into who you really are and how God individually wired you. And lastly, you may have some learned behaviors that are not part of your natural personality type but you have acquired them in order to function within your environment. For example, people tend to adopt some of the behaviors of their parents in order to thrive or survive in their families of origin. For example, Joan was a peaceful phlegmatic. However, she was raised in an environment where achievement, a powerful choleric trait, was valued over anything else. She learned to base her sense of self-worth on her productivity and achievement because of her upbringing, when deep down, what she really valued was the strength of her relationships.

Tips for Improved Communication with People with Different Personalities

Popular Sanguines:
- make an effort to be interested in their stories
- don't crush their spirit
- praise them often
- provide opportunities for new adventures
- appreciate them for their creativity and energy

Perfect Melancholies:
- sensitivity to their schedule (ie. Email them to set up a meeting versus just stopping by their desk.)
- don't cut them off or finish their sentences
- come prepared with facts and documentation

- respect their need for order and solitude
- appreciate them for their attention to details

Powerful Cholerics:
- stick to the bottom line
- pick up your pace
- be succinct
- appreciate them for all their hard work
- give them a sound bite and allow them to jump in if they want more info

Peaceful Phlegmatics:
- encourage and appreciate them for who they are not what they do
- stay engaged; don't dismiss them because of their slower pace
- develop patience and good listening skills
- watch for positives and reinforce them with praise
- appreciate their even-keel approach

Tempering Your Personality

Popular Sanguines:
- Attempt to move out of your weaknesses
- Tell a story on yourself but then STOP
- Limit your wordiness and conversation (ie only tell half your stories and count to 20 before you jump into the conversation)
- Because it's easy for Popular Sanguines to become the hero/heroine of the story, make a point of including others; be more interested than interesting, and look for ways to draw others in by asking questions
- Tone down – purposefully whisper
- Put boundaries on yourself to stay on track by having a non-Sanguine accountability partner; create lists (practice by making a grocery list and sticking to it)
- Hesitate to take on jobs until you've looked at your

calendar and consulted your mate. It's easy to over-commit, especially if it sounds fun
- Aim for quiet dignity – you will never be a Perfect Melancholy, but you can work toward their strengths
- Develop a sensitivity to others by praying for compassion

Perfect Melancholy
- Lighten up
- Don't take life so seriously
- Ask God to strengthen your faith – He really is trustworthy – even in the details
- Because it is easy for Melancholies to become self-absorbed, look for ways to build others up, even if the task isn't finished or perfect
- Don't demand perfection of yourself or others – everyone including Perfect Melancholies is in need of grace
- Receive compliments graciously
- Give praise instead of criticism – don't allow criticism to come out of your mouth until you have shared a positive comment first
- Engage in bit sized projects – because Melancholies can get overwhelmed if the project is too big, concentrate on one thing, finish it and move on
- Don't get stuck preparing – get started! Set deadlines for how long you will work on something and then stick to them

Powerful Choleric
- Remember, communication is about more than just the facts – it's also about *how* you come across to others
- Be interested in others – let them complete their own sentences and stories – don't assume that you know what they're going to say
- Broaden your horizons so you know something about something else besides what you're interested in
- Because Powerful Cholerics are so focused on production

and accomplishment, they can often run over others. Focus on the person and not just the task. See people for their intrinsic value, not for how they can help you accomplish your goals
- Cultivate the art of small talk. Take time to smell the roses and then talk to others about the experience
- Slow down – your brisk manner can often make you seem unapproachable and perpetually "too busy"
- Ask rather than demand. Asking makes people feel valued; demanding makes them feel devalued
- Be mindful of your tone of voice. You probably sound harsher than you intend to
- Crossing the finish line *alone* does not always make you the winner
- Let people see your heart – your efficiency and competence will be easy for others to see. Your heart may not be

Peaceful Phlegmatic
- Speak up and enter the conversation – practice speaking louder and more quickly
- Show enthusiasm with your body language
- Have an opinion – practice making and expressing choice
- Communicate your feelings so others can relate to you
- Learn some phrases that will encourage others – practice the etiquette of 'rejoicing with those who rejoice'
- Don't procrastinate or let others do your work
- Don't be a wet blanket on other's ideas – model a winner's attitude
- Find your real interest and pursue it
- Trust your own abilities and focus on your strengths instead of your weaknesses
- Speak the truth in love – don't always hold back, say what you mean and don't let resentment build up. It will come out as sarcasm in your witty one liners
- Involve yourself in other's lives

Meet the Author

Cindy Martin is a Writer, Speaker, and Certified Personality Trainer who has a heart for helping people get unstuck in their lives. She is passionate about teaching others how to live beyond their circumstances. She loves when people are able to understand the difference Jesus makes in their lives … everyday. Her vulnerability and authenticity about her life experiences combined with her love for God and His Word allow her to provide practical, biblical insights into the real issues of life. Her engaging and humorous style in tandem with her passion for prayer help her to forge deep connections with those interacts with—both individually and as a guest speaker.

She holds a Bachelor's degree in Religious Education and has completed a Master's Course in Disability and Suffering with Joni & Friends International. Cindy is also a CLASS (Christian Leaders, Authors & Speakers) and UpperCLASS graduate. She has completed her advanced certification as a Personality Trainer. Cindy loves reading, great conversations with friends, and going for walks by the creek with her husband Walter on their acreage near Calgary, AB in Canada. They have two adult children.

Cindy's passion finds its expression in her speaking, writing and teaching. For more information, visit www.lifemeetsreality.com.

You can also contact Cindy at cindy@lifemeetsreality.com.

ENDNOTES

CHAPTER ONE

1. http://www.answers.com
2. http://www.biblegateway.com/keyword (based on NIV translation)
3. *Webster's New Encyclopedic Dictionary*, New York: Black Dog & Levanthal, 1994. p. 462
4. John Walvoord & Roy Zuck, *The Bible Knowledge Commentary* Wheaton: Victor Books., p. 914
5. Quoted by Paul Brandt at Centre Street Church, Calgary, Alberta on October 24, 2010
6. *Webster's New Encyclopedic Dictionary*, p. 462

CHAPTER TWO

7. Flaaten, Rosemary, *A Woman and her Relationships* Kansas City: Beacon Hill Press, 2007.

CHAPTER THREE

8. Nelson, Alan. *Embracing Brokenness.* Colorado Springs: NavPress, 2002. p. 63
9. Ibid.
10. Spangler, *Anne. Becoming a Woman of Peace* Carol Stream, Illinois: Tyndale House Publisher, Inc., 2012, January 13.
11. Omartian, Stormie. *Choose Love.* Eugene, Oregon: Harvest House Publishers, 2014. p. 72

CHAPTER FOUR

12. Moore, Beth., *Breaking Free Bible Study* Lifeway:Nashville, 2009, p. 77
13. Cloud, Dr. Henry, *Integrity* Harper: New York, 2006., p.17

CHAPTER FIVE

14. Eareckson Tada, Joni. Beside Bethesda. NavPress, 2014. p. 35-37.

CHAPTER SIX

15. Omartian, Stormie. *The Prayer That Changes Everything; The Hidden Power of Praising God.* Harvest House Publishers, Oregon, 2004, p. 9,10
16. Ibid, Pages 16, 17
17. Ibid, Page 17
18. Ibid, Page 116
19. Ibid., p. 128
20. Ibid., p. 176
21. Ibid.,p. 169
22. Spangler, Ann. *The One Year Devotions for Women – Becoming a Woman at Peace.* Tyndale House Publishers, Carol Stream, Illinois, 2012, March 20.
23. Omartian, p. 163
24. Ibid, p. 31-33

CHAPTER SEVEN

25. *Wired That Way*, Florence & Marita Littauer, Regal Books, p.108

CHAPTER EIGHT

26. Cloud, Dr. Henry & Townsend, Dr. John, *Boundaries.* Zondervan Publishing House, Grand Rapids, Michigan, 1992., p. 134
27. Stanley, Charles. *Landmines in the Path of the Believer.* Nashville, Tennessee: Thomas Nelson 2008.
28. Cloud, Dr. Henry & Townsend, Dr. John, *Boundaries.* Zondervan Publishing House, Grand Rapids, Michigan, 1992., p. 263
29. Omartian, Stormie. *The Prayer That Changes Everything. The Hidden Power Of Praise.* Harvest House Publishers, Eugene, Oregon, 2004., p. 234.
30. DeMoss, Nancy Leigh. *The Quiet Place – Daily Devotional Readings* Moody Press, Chicago, 2012. July 5

31. Ibid., July 19
32. Ibid.
33. Omartian, p. 237.
34. Ibid
35. Cloud & Townsend, p. 264
36. DeMoss, May 2
37. DeMoss, May 3
38. DeMoss, May 4
39. Cloud & Townsend, p. 251
40. DeMoss, May 5
41. Cloud & Townsend, p. 263
42. DeMoss, May 5
43. Cloud & Townsend, p. 134.
44. Catherine Ponder (www.thinkexist.com)
45. Cloud & Townsend, p. 263
46. DeMoss, March 1
47. Ibid.
48. Ibid., October 22
49. Cloud & Townsend, p. 251
50. Omartian, p. 235
51. Moore, Beth. *Breaking Free, Updated Edition.* Nashville: LifeWay Church Resources, 2009, p. 211.
52. Omartian, p. 238
53. Spangler, Ann. *The One Year Devotions For Women – Becoming a Woman of Peace.* Carol Stream, Illinois: Tyndale House Publishers, Inc., 2012, April 5.

CHAPTER NINE
54. Ramsey, Dave. *Financial Peace Revisted.* Penguin Group: New York, New York. 2003., p. 27.
55. Ibid., p. 29
56. Ibid.

CHAPTER TEN
57. http://kacinicole.com/blog-galapagos/2016/7/17/the-cost-of-busyness
58. Ibid.
59. DeMoss, Nancy Leigh. *The Quiet Place*. Chicago: Moody Publishers, 2012., December 29.
60. https://michaelhyatt.com/more-margin.html, June 25, 2012
61. Young, Sarah. *Jesus Lives*, Nashville, TN, Thomas Nelson,2009. p. 156.

CHAPTER ELEVEN
62. Foster, Richard. *Celebration of Discipline*. San Francisco: HarperOne, 1998.
63. Tripp, Paul David. *New Morning Mercies: A Daily Gospel Devotional.* Wheaton, Illinois: Crossway, 2014, March 3.

CHAPTER TWELVE
64. Moore, Beth, *Breaking Free, The Journey, The Stories*. Updated Version Nashville, Tennessee: Lifeway Press, 2009., p.213
65. Ibid.
66. Ibid., p. 212
67. Omartian, Stormie. *The Prayer That Changes Everything. The Hidden Power Of Praise*. Harvest House Publishers, Eugene, Oregon, 2004., p. 22.
68. Ibid., p. 216
69. Young, Sarah, *Jesus Always* Nashville, Tennessee: Thomas Nelson, 2016., p. 104.
70. Omartian, p. 303
71. Omartian, p. 48.
72. Ibid.
73. Ibid., p. 133
74. Public Domain